AGAINST THE GRAIN

THE DILEMMA OF PROJECT FOOD AID
by Tony Jackson with Deborah Eade

CONTENTS

ACKNOWLEDGEMENTS

So many people have helped me bring out this book that it is impossible to thank them all by name. Indeed some of them in Europe, the United States and in certain developing countries have asked to remain anonymous.

My thanks go to them and the following: James Boyce and Betsy Hartmann whose friendship and knowledge of the subject kept me going – they also came up with the title; Elaine Edgcomb, Karen Funk and Helena Stalson who were a constant help and made me feel this was all worthwhile; Robert Gersony and Jo and Max Froman without whom there would be no report; Mary Day Kent, Steve Blythe, Paul Ensor, Carolyn Rhodes, Otto Matzke, Edward Clay, Julius Holt and Jane Pryer who all played important roles at various times; Brenda Parsons who spent many hours voluntarily typing for me in Boston; George Ann Potter for all her help and advice during my trip to Haiti and the Dominican Republic, and Laura Ziegler who worked on this project as a volunteer for six months and carried it along at crucial stages.

I owe OXFAM-America and its staff a great debt of gratitude for many services including their splendid hospitality while I did the early research.

Field workers provided much of my understanding about food aid and among them I would particularly like to mention Roland Bunch, Maria Colemont, Robert Grose, Jon Rohde and Denice Williams.

Officials from AID, CARE, Caritas, CRS, CWS, the EEC, FAO and WFP spent hours answering my questions and showed lots of kindness and patience towards me. I welcome this opportunity to thank them publicly. Staff of the American Friends Service Committee, the Mennonite Central Committee and World Neighbors also helped me to understand the issues as did members of Clark University in Worcester, Massachusetts.

Comments on various drafts were received and appreciated from many, among them Siegfried Bethke, Jonathan Fryer, Roger Hay, Pip Leitch, Simon Maxwell, Hans Singer, Alan Taylor, Charles Weitz and members of OXFAM advisory panels and staff, while Deborah Eade helped clarify my thinking and put it into Queen's English. The improvements are theirs; the deficiencies and responsibility are mine.

My colleagues in OXFAM both here and overseas were an unfailing source of encouragement and advice and the typing pool dealt efficiently and willingly with hundreds of pages of drafts. Finally Anthony Hawkins and Laura Hamilton helped proof-read the entire text.

My thanks to you all.

FOREWORD

Some 90,000 of our fellow human beings die every day from starvation or malnutrition. Behind that obscene statistic lies infinite human suffering and tragedy. Together with many other agencies, OXFAM has a long record of helping thousands of the people who face this frightening prospect. This time-honoured work represents part of our contribution to the relief of human suffering, which remains the centrepiece of our terms of reference. OXFAM will continue to make that kind of response wherever we can.

It is clear, however, that in certain areas of work the indiscriminate or uncontrolled distribution of food aid can do far more harm than good.

This book tries to identify more clearly the issues at the centre of the dilemma. We draw on experiences from OXFAM's own field programme, together with those of other agencies, both governmental and non-governmental. Our purpose is to stimulate debate and discussion, leading we hope, to better planning and closer cooperation between agencies. Ultimately we all seek to help to create conditions in which no one on this planet need die of starvation or malnutrition.

Our analysis does not focus on government-to-government bulk supplies of food aid at concessionary rates. We have limited ourselves to food aid for disaster relief, and especially for development programmes such as food-for-work, mother and child health, and school feeding programmes. The conclusions we reach are disturbing. They pose a challenge to all of us.

The principle author of our study, and the person mainly responsible for the analysis, is Tony Jackson, whom I invited to make an investigation of project food aid and the problems we had encountered first in Guatemala after the 1976 earthquake and then further afield. This included time spent in the USA, researching the subject, working in consultation with relevant offices of the US Government, exchanging information with American-based agencies and then, later, repeating a similar pattern of investigation in Europe.

Throughout his investigation Tony Jackson has had direct access to details of the whole of OXFAM's overseas programme covering over 80 countries in the Third World. He has also received substantial and willing cooperation from many sister voluntary agencies in North America, Europe and the Third World.

He has been ably assisted, in particular, by Deborah Eade, Ken Westgate and Suzanne Blumhardt, all OXFAM staff members.

The views expressed in this analysis do not necessarily represent the final position of OXFAM in respect of every issue discussed, but may be taken as stating the broad thrust of our considered judgement in this difficult, but vitally important, field of human endeavour. Our intention is to stimulate debate leading to dynamic action in favour of the hungry and distressed.

Brian W. Walker
Director General

PREFACE

My interest in food aid began after the earthquake in Guatemala in 1976. On joining OXFAM there, my first job was to buy items of immediate necessity: some medical goods, then salt and sugar, coffee and *cal* (lime used for making *tortillas*). After ten days or so OXFAM stopped this type of first-aid assistance and, in common with most other agencies, began planning how to help people rebuild their houses.

At the time of the disaster there had just been a record harvest in Guatemala. Despite it, vast quantities of food aid were brought in from the United States, causing a variety of negative effects. I became interested in trying to find out why this happened and I talked with many of those involved in the decision to import the food aid. One day a field worker from one of the food agencies told me that what I had learnt up till then about food aid was 'just the tip of the iceberg' and claimed that the Guatemala experience was no mere anomaly. I decided to look further into the matter and since 1976 have visited food aid projects in the Caribbean and Peru, read hundreds of reports and interviewed or been in correspondence with scores of people dealing with food aid in countries all over the world.

One point quickly became clear. While much had been written on the large bulk deliveries of food aid provided on a government-to-government basis, little was commonly known about food aid used in programmes such as food-for-work, mother-child health and school feeding, called collectively 'project food aid'. Indeed it seemed to be assumed by policy makers that this approach was working well and that more food aid should be used to support it. Given that there were in fact many reports calling this assumption into question, I felt that a book looking at the last 25 years of experience with project food aid might fill an important gap.

The result is clearly a polemic. This proved inevitable after my own experiences with food aid and after reading so many reports and letters and listening to the accounts of field workers, all full of woeful descriptions about the impact of the food upon poor communities.

I have incorporated into the text as many comments from the specialists as possible in order to let readers see what helped bring me to my own conclusions. I have tried to use the quotations to illustrate the point under discussion or to summarise the reports from which they are taken. I have also tried to select quotations without taking them out of context and believe that they fairly reflect the views of those quoted.

In summary, I have come to conclude that food aid is best used for refugees and in emergencies when food itself is short. Most large scale programmes to use project food aid for development have proved ineffective either because they simply do not work or because more locally suitable and often cheaper methods exist. What follows therefore is not just a description of bureaucratic inefficiency that could easily be put right, nor a suggestion that OXFAM or I could use food aid on this scale any better in non-disaster times. Nor is the report an attempt to underestimate the administrative difficulties posed by food aid. Just making the necessary arrangements to get the food to the right place at the right time is a major challenge; to use it for development after that adds another complex set of difficulties rarely overcome.

The report tries to describe what happens to food aid when it arrives in the recipient country. As such it does not aim to assess donor motivations, such as surplus disposal or the political reasons for food aid. These aspects have been thoroughly examined in other works referred to in the bibliography and, after all, if food aid did improve the lives of the poor, it would be churlish to criticise it for impurity of motive.

OXFAM's experience over the years with food aid is instructive. When it was founded in 1942, it was in order to send food and medical supplies to children in war-torn Greece. Even in the 1950s providing food, or supporting other agencies that did so, was one of its primary tasks. By the early sixties, however, Oxfam realised that the need for this type of programme had greatly diminished and that a longer-term development approach, not food distribution, was required if the condition of the poor was to be improved.Over the last few years OXFAM has received many expressions of concern from its own field staff and others about the negative effects caused by food programmes.

It is against this personal and institutional background that **Against the Grain** has been written. It examines reports and evaluations about food aid — many of them from food agencies themselves — and provides a forum for field workers, whose views have up to now gone largely unheeded. The report does not pretend to be the last word on the subject but aims to open up a debate long stifled as to when and how project food aid can best be used and when it may do more harm than good.

Tony Jackson
April 1982

Note: Throughout this study $ = United States dollars.

The Third World's problems are often not due to lack of food. Even in disasters there may be food available locally. When an earthquake struck Guatemala farmers were enjoying a bumper harvest.

1 PROJECT FOOD AID

PROJECT FOOD AID: AN IRREPLACEABLE TOOL FOR DEVELOPMENT?

E very year well over £1,000,000,000 worth of food aid is sent to developing countries, mainly from the United States (US), the European Economic Community (EEC), Australia, Canada and Japan. (1) Approximately 70% of this is given or sold on concessional terms to Third World governments. (2) They usually sell it and use the proceeds from the sales to supplement their budgets: strictly speaking this is not food aid, but a form of government budgetary support. These government-to-government transactions have given rise to frequent, sometimes bitter, criticism, but they are not the subject of this report. By contrast, the remaining 30% of the food is designed to be distributed free of charge to the poor, either through long-term development projects or in relief operations after disasters and for refugee feeding. This is called **project food aid**, the effects of which will be examined in this report.

The kinds of projects which might be supported by this use of food aid range from those aimed at increasing local food production – such as land improvement schemes where food is used as a form of wages for paying the workers – to nutrition programmes involving mothers and their children where food supplements are distributed. In 1979 there were over 60,000,000 people receiving project food aid from the US alone. (3) Most project food aid is channelled through the World Food Programme (WFP) and the two major US voluntary agencies, CARE (Cooperative for American Relief Everywhere) and Catholic Relief Services (CRS). (See Appendix for thumbnail sketches of the donors.)

Whatever the obvious limitations of government-to-government aid, project food aid has generally been assumed to be working well and in the direct interests of the poor. Its overtly humanitarian functions have allowed it to go uncriticised and the fact that it is largely disbursed through the United Nations (UN) and voluntary agencies for 'development' purposes has served almost as a talisman against public criticism. Of course, it is admitted, project food aid has had its problems – some of it inevitably goes astray; it requires a considerable degree of logistic support and administrative control, and it is not easy to ensure that it arrives on time and in the right quantities. But such problems are usually dismissed as incidental to the food itself, administrative difficulties that will disappear once the project is properly under way.

Official confidence in project food aid is expressed in various ways. In 1975 the US Congress enacted a requirement that a certain minimum amount of food aid had to go each year under Title II of Public Law (PL) 480, that part of the law covering project food aid. (See Appendix for more details on PL 480.) By 1982, 1,700,000 metric tons must by law be distributed this way. (4) Frequent appeals by the Director-General of the Food and Agriculture Organization (FAO) have been made to ask the international community to donate more food through WFP, described on one occasion as follows:

> "Fully experienced and efficiently managed, WFP is the instrument *par excellence* for shipping food aid; in addition, it is an irreplaceable tool for development because 80 percent of its resources is allocated to development projects." (5)

Likewise the Brandt Commission report wholly endorses the idea of food aid for development:

> "Food aid should be increased and linked to employment promotion and agricultural programmes and projects without weakening incentives to food production." (6)

The concept of using food as a tool for development is superficially attractive, and receives widespread public support. Yet over the years there have been many criticisms made of it. Reports from numerous countries and projects have questioned the efficacy of project food aid. These disquieting reports have been noted, but general principles have largely not been drawn from them. In this book it is argued that the cumulative evidence points to the irresistible conclusion that large scale project food aid is an inherently inappropriate means of promoting development. In the 25 or so years it has been used, project food aid has in fact fallen disappointingly short of the development goals it has been set. Year after year, independent and commissioned evaluations have failed to find evidence of an improvement proportional to the vast amounts of food, money and human effort which have been expended.

In 1979, after field evaluations in six countries (Ghana, Tanzania, India, Sri Lanka, the Dominican Republic and Peru), the General Accounting Office of the Government of the US submitted a report to Congress stating that "fundamental changes are needed in the way title II [project food aid] is planned, programed, and administered at the country level", so calling for a complete overhaul of the policies governing project food aid. (7)

In 1980 a report to the Nordic Ministerial Council stated that "the whole issue of food aid remains an area of controversy, ambiguity and disorder". (8) In the same year, a working document prepared for the Committee on Development and Cooperation of the European Parliament, stated that the EEC food aid policy was

> "an inefficient way of distributing European surplus production to the poor countries, associated with high costs, countless mishaps, delays, wrangling over responsibility and bureaucratic obstacles; there is scarcely any control over how it works and what effects it achieves. . . Any attempt to hold it up to scrutiny leads to a radically different suggestion: confine food aid to emergency aid and otherwise replace it with financial assistance." (9)

A few weeks later, the Court of Auditors of the EEC echoed that assessment in its **Special Report on Community Food Aid**, finding that "programming and management of Community food aid needs to be completely recast". (10)

In a debate on development aid policy in June 1981, Lord Trefgarne, the Under-Secretary of State for Trade, told the House of Lords that the British Government had "reservations about the developmental benefits of food aid" and that it had consistently opposed increases in EEC dairy food aid. (11)

As far as voluntary agencies are concerned, in 1981 the World Council of Churches published a study critical of project food aid. (12) In the US, Church World Service (CWS), in partnership with Lutheran World Relief, have engaged a consultant to investigate the issue, while in 1980, in testimony to its parliament, the Canadian Council for International Co-operation, an umbrella group for 75 voluntary agencies, recommended that "except in cases of emergencies, food aid be abolished." (13)

Outside the development agencies there has been in recent years an unprecedented spate of unfavourable comment about project food aid in the world press, as well as television and radio coverage on both sides of the Atlantic.

This report seeks to investigate the impact of food aid as a tool for development. It does not therefore focus primary attention on arguments that have occasionally been made in its favour — for example that, even if it does go astray, at least it supplements the total amount of food available in the country. Clearly, agricultural disincentives aside, even misplaced food must make such a contribution. But the founding premise of project food aid is that it **can** be used discriminatingly, that it **can** be 'targeted' at 'needy individuals' in development programmes and that it **can** be a long-term development tool. These are the terms in which it is justified and, after 25 years, these are the criteria against which it should be judged.

This book is based largely on the published findings of the food aid institutions themselves and on independent evaluations carried out on behalf of the governments for whom the agencies act as custodians. It draws also upon academic and official surveys of the published material. Most importantly, it gives a platform to field workers, many of whom have had direct experience of handling food aid, as well as those who have been well placed to observe its effects both on the recipient communities as a whole, and on development projects in particular.

The book is divided into two sections. Chapters 2-5 examine the major mechanisms by which project food aid is distributed — disaster relief (including refugee feeding), food-for-work (FFW), mother-child-health (MCH) and school and other institutional feeding. These chapters draw upon case studies which show that what is happening in the field is often at odds with head office theory.

In disasters (Chapter 2), food aid is often sent and distributed in a haphazard and ill-planned way. Many calls for help are answered late or inappropriately; often there is no need to hand out the food free of charge and, sometimes, food may not be what is needed at all. To overcome such difficulties, the question of food aid in disasters needs to be much more closely examined.

Food-for-work programmes (Chapter 3) generally have a notoriously low productivity rate and are widely associated with shoddy workmanship, so that although they create short-term employment, their claim to provide long-term benefits to the community is often proved wrong. On occasions, the benefits

3

which are created accrue to the relatively well-off, some of whom get free labour provided under the FFW scheme. In such cases, there is more than a little truth in the aphorism that the rich get richer and the poor get food aid.

Mother and child health programmes distributing food (Chapter 4) have usually failed to improve nutritional levels and have also failed to reach those who are most in need of supervised supplementary feeding. In most cases attempts to provide nutrition education are no more than token. There is even some evidence that children who do **not** receive food aid do better nutritionally than those who do.

School feeding (Chapter 5) discriminates against the poor and the nutritionally most vulnerable; it is also subject to all the risks of unsupervised 'supplementary' feeding. Evaluations have not found that it has brought about lasting improvements in attendance rates.

In short, the evidence is that although the food may be feeding people, the beneficiaries are usually not those who are most in need. These chapters also challenge the commonly-held belief that food aid is a matter of life and death and that the poor are dependent on it. Most of the programmes provide a welfare service at best while the long-term development benefits have been slight.

The remaining chapters discuss the problems intrinsic and peculiar to food aid and the difficulties faced by development projects which are based on, or incorporate, distribution of free foreign food. The most obvious disadvantage, to both donors and recipients alike, is the high cost associated with food aid as it is currently administered (Chapter 6). This financial burden usually increases each year and causes the cost-benefit ratio to worsen. It is likely that many of the aims of project food aid could be achieved by cheaper means and without the risk of a programme's continued dependence on foreign food.

More crucial still is the unwieldiness of large-scale consignments of free food, which makes it extremely difficult to handle as an efficient development tool (Chapter 7). Losses through damage or misappropriation are rife and the lack of proper records, an affliction common to many food aid projects, means that often no one knows what has happened to the food at all, other than that someone has taken it away. Despite that, routine administration of the food still absorbs a disproportionate amount of field workers' time and attention, distracting them from the development component of the programme.

The effect of project food aid on local food production also needs to be considered. Most of the literature on this subject looks at government-to-government transactions as project food aid was assumed to be too small to have any serious disruptive effect. However, it is clear that free food can compete with local food in the market place and for storage and transport facilities. This aspect is examined in Chapter 8.

On the other hand, there is sometimes a need for controlled nutrition interventions using supplementary feeding, which may or may not require imported food, according to local circumstances. Strict monitoring and close observation would be an absolute pre-condition of such programmes, to ensure that the food supplements go only to those in real need and do not become substitutes for the normal diet. These provisos would disqualify the great majority of beneficiaries

4

of supplementary and school feeding programmes as they are currently adminis-tered.

Even more urgent is the need to give a much higher priority to food aid for relief after natural and man-made disasters. In 1980 food aid arrived late in both Uganda and Somalia with obvious human consequences, while thousands of tons were shipped elsewhere for less urgent programmes.

The overall conclusion is that long-term project food aid does not overcome the problems it sets out to solve, and can even exacerbate them. While some pro-grammes have successfully integrated food handouts with development work, these are very much the exception to the rule. In most cases the commodity dic-tates the programmes and the food aid tail wags the development dog. What food aid proponents fail to acknowledge is that in most cases project food aid applies a first-aid measure to a long-term disease. It ignores the fundamental problem which is poverty, and attempts to address the symptom, which is hunger. Poverty is an economic problem. The poor, by definition, lack money. It is the argument of this book that food aid is not an appropriate substitute.

Some of the food aid agencies have in the past been intensely hostile to criti-cism, yet the last 25 years also bear witness to the enormous fund of goodwill and humanitarian concern which these agencies have at their disposal. It is to be hoped that these strengths will be redirected to more fruitful ends.

When people seek refuge in a neighbouring country they can seriously strain the resources of their hosts. When they arrive in large numbers they may risk hunger or even death if food aid is not available.

2 FOOD AID FOR DISASTER RELIEF AND REFUGEES

O f any images spring to mind at the mention of food aid, they are those of emaciated children, the forlorn victims of natural disaster, or of refugees pathetically seeking asylum in countries which lack the resources to provide for them. In such cases, what could be more appropriate than countries with food surpluses offering humanitarian assistance in the form of donations of free food?

Yet of the £1,000,000,000 of food aid disbursed throughout the world each year, only about 10% is allocated to disaster relief. [1] Consequently, when food aid is desperately needed, it is often not readily available. When it does arrive, it may be inappropriate to people's needs, there may be too much or too little of it, there may be no adequate means of transporting it within the stricken country, or, more tragically, it may simply be too late. On many occasions, well-intentioned efforts have caused more problems than they have solved.

The first part of this chapter will examine individual case-studies of disaster relief programmes under three main headings:

When is food aid needed?

How should it be distributed?

When should the food aid stop?

The second part will look at some of the policies of the food aid donors governing emergency supplies and at the suggestions that have been made to improve them.

When is Food Aid Needed?

Some disasters affect food availability; these include drought and flooding, both of which may disrupt local and regional food production for a time. Subsistence farming communities may be seriously affected by such environmental vagaries and forced to compete in local markets for food, if they have the resources to do so. Landless labourers and small farmers working in the cash crop sector of the economy require the food market for their survival. However, when food production falls, prices rise and access to the market becomes difficult for the poor. Seeds are often eaten instead of being planted. So, in these food-related disasters food aid, both in the short-term and the medium-term, may be required.

Other disasters, such as hurricanes or earthquakes, may bring about a temporary shortage of local foods if crops are damaged or roads are destroyed. A recovery can usually be made soon afterwards. Thus food aid will be needed, if at all, for a limited period only.

In the case of 'man-made' disasters (such as wars and civil disturbances), which involve refugees, a large influx of people who are not producing food may seriously stretch the local market. At these times, food will have to be imported by the host country; in many cases, food aid will be required.

It is relatively easy to see what damage has been done in a sudden-impact disaster, such as an earthquake or flood, and what the needs for food or other assistance might be. Interventions in cases of drought and consequent famine are harder to judge. In addition, the governments of affected countries may be reluctant to release details of the catastrophe to the international community — aid agencies are obliged to wait for their host government's approval before they publicise the need for action.

The results of such a policy are best illustrated by the case of Ethiopia in the early 1970s where the relief operation only began in earnest long after the famine had started. For political reasons the international community felt obliged to refrain from making public statements about its extent as long as the Government itself did not do so and made no appeal for help. Starvation followed. (2)

In other cases official inertia appears to have caused a lack of response. The Sahelian drought of the late 1960s and early 70s caused thousands of deaths; the number is unknown but the usual estimate is about 100,000. (3) It was not until 1973, **six years** after the famine began, however, that large-scale relief efforts started. The facts were known to the international community but little action was taken before the worst effects of the drought had been felt and tens of thousands had died. A report from the Carnegie Endowment for International Peace comments:

> "The catastrophe of the drought did not happen suddenly. For at least four years, scores of officials from the U.S. and the U.N. were in the region, observing that the states of the Sahel were essentially helpless to deal with the drought, reporting the gathering disaster, and dispensing some relief. Yet neither the U.S. nor the U.N. had contingency plans to deal with the tragedy as it reached overwhelming proportions by the fall of 1972." (4)

It would be a mistake, however, to assume that simply to send supplies of food to the stricken country will solve the problem. Unless care is taken, the logistical problems associated with freight, storage and distribution of perishable commodities can create an administrative burden that is too great for the local infrastructure to sustain. This can cause difficulties for the recipient country.

> "Following a drought in 1972/3, Britain offered Lesotho emergency food aid. The Lesotho response was that it could absorb 1,000 tons of wheat. However, when a firm offer came from the UK it was for 6,000 tons of wheat. The Lesotho Government accepted the increased amount even though adequate storage facilities did not exist, and at the same time received as emergency food aid over 1,000 tons of Belgian wheat flour instead of the 662 tons originally requested, as well as its normal development food aid deliveries. In addition, and con-

trary to expectation, the 1973/4 harvest was particularly large. The result was the diversion of Lesotho government personnel away from the management of routine food aid into the task of finding ways of storing and disposing of the surplus wheat, the construction of 6 new storage sheds at a cost of R45,000 [about £27,500], and the loss through rotting of many bags of wheat." [5]

At the more local level, careful planning and supervision are essential if incidents such as the following are to be avoided. The first is from a study of food distribution in Uganda.

"Respondents complained that the food aid had only been distributed from one to four times since mid-1980, in most but not all communities. Nothing was distributed anywhere in North Teso during November and December, 1980, and most respondents were doubtful that distributions would be resumed. The quantities handed out were usually so small and the distributions so chaotic (one local porter was killed and six injured during one distribution at Katakwi after they were allegedly thrown off a truck by CARE employees escaping from a dissatisfied crowd), that many residents considered the whole operation totally ineffective." [6]

A correspondent who worked in Haiti in the mid-1970s described the difficulties of drought-relief food aid as follows:

"In Haiti we had much more of a problem of theft and mishandling. In [a] town... fairly near to us and very badly hit by drought, the magistrate (appointed mayor) was known to sell PL480 food for $7.00 a 50 lb. bag. At other times the CARE food distributers were so desperate that they would just throw bags of food off the truck and drive on so that the food would go to the strong and the swift." [7]

In other cases, imported food may not be necessary at all, despite a major disaster, and its arrival may do more harm than good. The classic example of this comes from Guatemala where the earthquake in 1976 killed an estimated 23,000 people, injured over three times as many and left a million and a quarter homeless. The earthquake occurred in the middle of a record harvest. Local grain was plentiful and the crops were not destroyed but left standing in the fields or buried under the rubble but easy to recover.

During the first few weeks, small consumer items — salt, sugar, *cal,* soap etc. — were in short supply and temporarily unavailable in the shops. Some of these small items, such as salt, were lost when the houses collapsed. People expressed a need for these food items in the short period before commercial supplies were resumed. However, during that year, about 25,400 tons of basic grains and blends were brought in as food aid from the US. A further 5,000 tons of US food aid already stored in Guatemala were released and supplies were also sent in from elsewhere in the region. [8]

CRS and CARE both received reports from their field staff saying food aid was not needed. The Director of CARE's housing reconstruction programme visited the disaster area soon after the earthquake. In a US Government report he stated:

> "Another thing I was really concerned with was whether there was any need to import food or seed. But I saw no indication of that whatsoever. First of all, the earth was not damaged, and there was no reason why the crops couldn't be harvested on time, and I believe it was a good crop that year. Also, in a few places I visited, I asked people if they could pull the food they had in their houses out of the rubble, and they said they certainly could." (9)

CRS field staff objected to the importing of food aid but they were overruled by their headquarters in New York. (10) Two weeks after the disaster, the League of Red Cross Societies asked national Red Cross Societies to stop sending food. As early as February (the same month as the earthquake), the Co-ordinator of the National Emergency Committee of the Government of Guatemala asked voluntary agencies to stop imports of food aid. (11) On 4 March, the Assistant Administrator for the Latin America Bureau of the United States Agency for International Development (AID), the Hon. Herman Kleine, testified before a House of Representatives Sub-Committee.

> "I should like to add here, Mr. Chairman, that the Guatemalan Government has requested officially to all donors that further inkind contributions not be of food and medicine but roofing and building materials." (12)

Finally, the Government of Guatemala invoked a presidential decree to prohibit imports of basic grains from May 1976 onwards. (13) Yet after this decree, quantities of food aid were still imported in the form of **blended** foodstuffs. One article refers to these blends as "basic grains in disguise". (14)

Field staff and local leaders identified three negative results. Firstly, they considered that food aid contributed to a drop in the price of local grain that occurred soon after the earthquake and continued throughout 1976. As to the need for basic grains, a peasant farmer explained:

> "There was no shortage. There was no need to bring food from outside. On the contrary, our problem was to sell what we had." (15)

After an extensive survey of towns and villages in the worst-hit area six weeks after the earthquake, an OXFAM-World Neighbors official reported:

> "Virtually everyone in the area is selling more grain this year than he does normally. Furthermore, emergency food shipments have drastically curtailed demand for grains. Thus the prices of the farmers' produce have plummeted." (16)

Later, the then Director of CRS in Guatemala was to tell the New York Times:

"The general effect was that we knocked the bottom out of the grain market in the country for nine to twelve months." (17)

This last view may be overstated as other factors, such as the excellent grain harvest, would usually have led to a fall in prices anyway. Nonetheless, the basic fact remains: $8 million of food aid was sent into a country with plentiful food-stocks of its own. Any food that it was necessary to distribute to earthquake victims could have been bought in Guatemala (as WFP did).

The second negative effect of the continuing supply of free food was to encourage the survivors to queue for rations instead of engaging in reconstruction or normal agricultural work. (18)

Thirdly, it brought about a change in the quality and motivation of local leadership. The OXFAM-World Neighbors official, quoted above, noted:

"Immediately after the earthquake, we tended to see the same leaders whom we'd seen before the earthquake – people . . . [with] a high degree of honesty and personal commitment to the villages. But gradually . . . . I began seeing fellas who I knew were totally dishonest. They'd go into the different agencies and . . . . say that theirs was the most affected village in the Highlands, and they'd get more food. So largely because of the give-aways, the villages started to turn more to leaders who could produce free things like this, whether they were honest or dishonest, rather than to the leaders they'd been putting their trust in for years.

With larger and larger quantities of free food coming in, there are increased incentives to corruption. . . . Groups that had worked together previously became enemies over the question of recipients for free food." (19)

If at times food aid has been distributed when the need for it did not exist, at others it has been sent in too late to be of use and has therefore been wasted. In Haiti, much of the food aid for the drought in 1977 failed to arrive until 1978 and was distributed during and after a very good harvest in the drought area. A UN official in Haiti stated that the reason food aid was given out when it was no longer needed was that it was "not economically feasible" to send it back again. (20) What happened in Haiti has since been dismissed as an anomaly. (21) Yet similar events have taken place elsewhere.

— A WFP relief programme aimed at vulnerable groups in Bangladesh, such as small children and pregnant and nursing mothers, began in January 1976, more than a year after the outbreak of famine. (22)

— EEC skimmed milk powder requested by Grenada after flooding in 1976 arrived in 1979, in time for another emergency. (23)

— US food aid for the famine of 1977-78 in Bas Zaire arrived in the latter part of July 1979, many months after the crisis had passed. (24)

— In April 1980, the EEC sent over 500 tons of rice and 100 of butteroil to Dominica, although the need for food aid caused by the 1979 hurricanes had long passed. (25)

It must be recognised that after a certain delay has occurred, the food commitments cannot provide effective emergency relief and that a large influx of free food after that point may serve to cause problems by interrupting the local economy and interfering with recovery efforts. Such belated consignments of food should, therefore, be cancelled.

Thus, when food aid is needed, it is important to ensure that it arrives on time and in the right quantities. When food crops have been damaged or destroyed by adverse weather, the likely shortfall can often be predicted some time in advance of any hardship. Similarly, in the case of refugee communities, food needs can often be forecast. Although the timing of interventions may be difficult to judge, donors could make greater efforts to anticipate food aid requirements and to negotiate with potential recipient governments. This would reduce the crucial delays which occur between the decision to intervene and the eventual delivery of food consignments. In the case of food aid for sudden-impact disasters, speed is important.

A well-organised and equitable relief programme **is** possible. In the devastated south-west of the Dominican Republic following Hurricanes David and Frederick in 1979, food-stocks were largely destroyed. An appeal was relayed to Caritas of Holland and food aid, paid for by the Dutch, was immediately sent in by sea from other Caribbean islands and 8 weeks later from Holland itself. WFP also transferred stocks from Haiti. The swift international response enabled food to meet the needs of 300,000 people over a five-month period. From the beginning, recipients were told that the food would be provided only for these five months; thus, the false expectations of continued food assistance were not created and no institutionalisation of the programme followed. The programme was designed and run locally and its success was largely due to these factors. (26)

What Kind of Food?

Once the vulnerable groups have been identified, actual requirements must be determined to ensure that the rations suit individual needs and that the total donations do not upset local marketing arrangements. It is doubtful whether potato crisps, slimming foods, 'Ribena' or spaghetti sauce (seen as food aid in Chad, Guatemala, Kampuchea and the Dominican Republic) could ever be a suitable form of assistance.

The consequences of sending inappropriate food can be serious. During the Biafran War of 1968, large quantities of Emmenthaler cheese were sent from Switzerland.

"As it happened, the population drank extremely little milk in normal times and cheese was virtually unknown. The adults would not even taste it, whilst children dutifully swallowed a few mouthfuls and then vomited. The relief workers themselves discovered that they had limited appetites for the stuff, and when storage of the sweating cheese became too difficult it had to be buried." (27)

Where there is a need for medically supervised nutrition interventions, protein-fortified foods may be especially useful; but for general supplementary feeding programmes, the chief need is for a high calorie intake. Yet vast amounts of dried skimmed milk (which has a **low** calorie content) have been donated for disaster relief programmes even in countries where people have a lactose intolerance and where the "extensive infrastructure of health services" needed to ensure its safe use, cannot be provided. (28)

One way of ensuring the suitability of food aid is to purchase it locally or regionally wherever possible. This is an approach to disaster relief which is increasingly favoured by both the EEC and the WFP. The EEC refers to this method as 'triangular operations' because it makes money available to buy food in a country near to the afflicted area rather than sending out food of its own. (29) In fact, food is usually locally or regionally available, as one experienced field worker has reported.

> "We found in all the major disasters that there was always enough food in the surrounding area to take care of the needs. There was never a need to import foods from the industrialized countries. The surrounding area can be broadly defined. But let's say that in Managua there was enough food in Nicaragua. In Guatemala, if there had really been a need for it, there would have been enough food in Central America. For Biafra, there was enough food in the neighboring countries. After the war, there was enough in Nigeria to meet the Biafrans' needs. There was also enough food in the area around Bangladesh. Very rarely after a disaster do you need to import foods at all." (30)

It is important to make an accurate assessment of food requirements before food aid, from wherever it comes, is dispatched. (31) These requirements are determined by various factors, such as whether the food aid is intended as a **supplement** (because of local crop failure, perhaps) or whether it will be the only food supply. A report by a former FAO Food and Nutrition Adviser shows how vitally important this assessment can be.

> "During April 1978 and the following months some 200,000 refugees from Burma streamed into Bangladesh and a massive relief programme with international assistance was started. In spite of the fact that the help which was offered exceeded the needs, as many as 10,000 people (7,000 of them children) died by the end of the year . . . . Of the 10,000 people who died in this case, some 7,000-8,000 should under normal circumstances have survived." (32)

Though the required food was available, "an artificial famine-like situation developed with massive malnutrition and excessive mortality". (33) The ration had been determined incorrectly by calculating what the Government gave its own people in times of disaster; this was not a full ration but a supplementary one, as settled communities are very rarely entirely without food of their own. Unfortunately, after the first few weeks, the refugees had to exist entirely on food aid. Thus, the food provided was too little. The author of the report concludes by deploring the lack of systematic guidelines for calculating food needs, saying that,

> "It is well known that similar relief disasters have happened before and that they may happen again. . . One of the most striking features [of the present system] is the lack of agreed norms and recommendations related to food provision and established human nutritional needs. . . Lack of clarity on this basic point leaves room for indecision and fumbling which can have disastrous consequences." (34)

The food requirements of a stricken community should, as far as possible, be established before commitments are made from overseas. Systematic checks of regionally available supplies would, in many cases, indicate that needs could be partially or entirely satisfied from within the area. This approach is recommended since it not only helps to ensure that donations are compatible with the normal diet but also reduces transport costs and is quicker, as well as being of economic benefit to the country in which the purchases are made.

How Should Food Aid Be Distributed?

In emergencies, the most pressing need is to distribute the food speedily and equitably. Sometimes, this can be done through institutions (such as schools or hospitals) or development programmes already in existence. It may be, however, that there is no infrastructure adequate to cope with the food, that existing projects refuse to handle it, or that the stricken area is unfamiliar territory to the food aid agencies. Any of these factors can make it difficult to distribute the food fairly, and can increase the likelihood of its being given to all-comers, regardless of individual need.

All of the above factors were reflected in the Karamoja relief operation of 1980-81. The Karamoja district had long been regarded as a Ugandan backwater; for a variety of reasons, development agencies had little knowledge of either the region or its society.

When the news of the famine came to the attention of the outside world, much of the damage had already been done and the relief work which ensued was something of a salvage operation. Nonetheless, insecurity in the area, combined with confusion, mismanagement and bureaucratic obstacles on the part of the various agencies of the UN meant that there were even more delays in delivering and distributing adequate food supplies. (35) In addition, accurate population figures were not available.

Food was meant to be supplied to families through FFW projects and supplementary feeding centres for mothers and children. Some effective relief work was done and undoubtedly lives were saved. However, many OXFAM field workers commented on the fact that irregular and unreliable supplies strained their working relationship to the utmost, particularly since food had at first been distribut-

14

ed indiscriminately. An OXFAM official, who had lived in Uganda for some time before the relief programmes started, reported as follows:

> "[The Karamojong] are quite capable of killing you if they think you're ripping them off and that's why the food's got to get here on time." (36)

An OXFAM official working in another part of Uganda reported:

> "Food for work has never taken off the ground here and it is difficult to see how that could change now — people are used to their ration for nothing and they get very upset if it is fiddled about. But [there is] no famine now — population figures to which we are working are probably up to twice the actual size." (37)

There was the additional problem about conflicting, if not contradictory, approaches to food distribution. For example, a UNICEF nutrition officer certified that the children in one feeding centre were not suffering from malnutrition; the OXFAM field worker, therefore, closed it down. In spite of this, another agency then organised feeding centres in the same area which, it was observed, continued to undermine family structures that had already been severely weakened. (38)

There were also managerial problems. The difficulty of ascertaining accurate population figures has already been mentioned. This, together with the urgency associated with relief operations, meant that officials who went to take over the programme found that records were inadequate and that unaccounted losses were rife.

> "I started to sort out the mess of the stores and the accounting system which was non-existent, in that the figures that were produced bore no relation to the actual stock. . . . One of the weakest links in the supply chain from Tororo to Moroto was that ¡the lorries left Tororo without an escort, so that a fair percentage of the loads never actually arrived, the load was sold in Mbale, then the lorry went to Soroti to the CARE warehouse and reloaded before going on to Moroto." (39)

Many of these problems are frequent in **long-term** projects using food aid but the consequences can be particularly grave in **relief** work. While it is impossible to generalise about distribution methods as circumstances vary considerably, the Karamoja experience does serve to highlight some of the pitfalls common to relief operations.

The most important is that feeding centres run the risk of becoming permanent settlements which draw people away from the rural areas, where they might resume food production. (40) This tacitly condones the idea that help has to come from outside. An agency has to balance these risks against its ability to handle the distribution of food aid efficiently and effectively.

As noted earlier, a famine does not always mean that there is no local food available. The case of the 1974 famine in Bangladesh is a most telling example of

15

the distinction between food availability and distribution. The common view is that floods were responsible for food shortages and, therefore, famine. 1974, however, was a peak year, both for total rice production and output per head in Bangladesh. (41)) Employment opportunities, on the other hand, **were** curtailed by the floods, as the following article describes:

> "Taking wheat production and imports into account, there was no decline in the availability of food grains. Employment opportunities, however, did diminish as a result of the floods and this decline in the demand for labour was accompanied by a fall in the wage rate relative to the price of rice. In one district the 'rice entitlement of wages' fell by up to 70 percent. Once again, the incidence of famine was highest among labourers." (42)

In fact it may not always be necessary to provide very much additional food to prevent starvation. An AID official, who was working in Bangladesh in 1974, later wrote that,

> "The early allocation of food for people affected by the flood could have been accomplished with relatively small amounts of grain. If 2,000 tons of grain had been promptly allocated to the northwest, starvation could have been prevented." (43)

Field workers have also commented on the changes in local attitudes to rehabilitation work or to development projects which can follow in the wake of prolonged distribution of free food.

> "Food distribution programs make future development work which does not involve free goods much more difficult. . . . People with long-term development programs in Honduras have complained that, since Hurricane Fifi and the emergency effort which followed it, long-term nutrition and agricultural programs have been practically impossible because the people are only interested in what those from the outside are willing to give them." (44)

The OXFAM Field Director for South India noticed a similar trend after a cyclone in Andhra Pradesh.

> "Even in Divi, where relief was needed, continued distribution of free food and supplies became counter-productive. Villagers came to find it more attractive to sit by the roadside waiting for distribution than to go back to work." (45)

One alternative would be to **sell** the food aid. When food is sold, even at subsidised prices, the onus for selection lies with the purchasers; they decide whether or not they wish to take advantage of the scheme.

Sales would not have been possible in Kampuchea, in 1979/80 where money had been destroyed by the Khmer Rouge and food was used to pay city-workers. In many other cases, however, there is no need to give the food away in this

16

manner; a shortage of food does not necessarily mean that people have no money. In Karamoja, for example, food aid could have been sold in the same way as seeds and other agricultural inputs were under an OXFAM project. (46)

In Guatemala, the OXFAM/World Neighbours project sold food aid (salt, sugar, etc.) and reconstruction materials to the stricken villagers. The money thus generated enabled more relief supplies to be bought — a system which the recipients regarded as equitable. (47) Sales of subsidised relief supplies have also been sponsored by AID in similar circumstances. (48) The EEC sent emergency food aid to Cape Verde which was sold in order to create more cash-paid employment; people were thus enabled to buy food and other needs as they required. (49) In the Dominican Republic in 1979, the food aid supplied through a locally-organised relief group was sold at subsidised prices, the proceeds being used to pay for the cost of the programme. (50) Sales of food do, of course, need to be carefully controlled to avoid abuses, such as bulk-buying by individuals. This was done in all the above examples.

The sales approach does not preclude the setting up of medically controlled nutrition rehabilitation units for those people who might otherwise be missed but who are in need of special treatment; these clinics would act as a useful indicator of the food needs of the local community.

Finally, one of the greatest advantages of the organised selling of relief supplies, apart from the increased level of accountability this introduces, is that the food aid does not compromise the future relationship between the aid worker and the local people, or set up false expectations of subsequent development projects.

When Should Relief Food Aid Stop?

In general, development agencies and field workers are agreed that it is undesirable as well as unnecessary to prolong the distribution of free food after a disaster. This is illustrated by a series of reports made by the local Caritas office following the drought in Haiti in 1977.

"It is the wish of all conscientious leaders that we should stop receiving food from outside. . . More or less everywhere in the diocese there are complaints that food aid is harming community spirit." (51)

Three months later, the office stated:

"In our opinion, food aid, although necessary for the survival of the population, does not cease to pose serious problems. Community spirit is diminishing and corruption installing itself in the hearts of those immediately in charge." (52)

Three months later still, when production was coming in after the rains, they reported:

"At last we hope to rid ourselves of the yoke of imported food which has no other effect than of diminishing community spirit, while encouraging passivity in people." (53)

17

Donors, however, are very anxious to integrate emergency food relief with long-term development work. As the former Executive-Director of WFP wrote in his Annual Report for 1980:

"First, emergency food aid should be provided speedily but for a relatively short period of time, sufficient, however, to attend to the most urgent and basic needs. Secondly, emergency assistance should be phased out as quickly as possible and a programme of reconstruction and rehabilitation supported as a bridge to fully-fledged developmental action." (54)

Since the WFP uses food aid in all its "developmental actions" it is not easy to see what exactly the practical distinction between these and the projects which involve "emergency food aid" is — except that the work planned in FFW programmes may be more permanent.

Development work often originates as disaster relief. However, the problem with projects which have their roots in relief food hand-outs is, as already noted, that it can prove difficult to move towards a more self-reliant form of development. There are several factors which contribute to this institutionalisation of food-aid projects.

Firstly, food aid both for emergency relief and development work is, in most cases, distributed by the same groups and through the same channels. It is, therefore, extremely easy to drift from one to the other.

For example, since the earthquake of 1976, Guatemala has continued to receive much larger amounts of non-disaster food aid than it had ever received before. (55) This is not uncommon.

— Food aid was first sent to Haiti in 1954 after Hurricane Hazel. As one priest commented, "It simply never stopped coming". (56)

— Food aid to Lesotho began in 1962 for emergency relief and, by 1978, 10% of the nation's food was being imported and distributed by CRS and WFP. By 1979, about half the population was a recipient of US project food aid. (57)

— Food aid from West Germany to the People's Republic of Yemen began in 1972 as emergency aid. Afterwards, it continued at the same level — as project food aid. (58)

Secondly, the accurate targeting and distribution of free food requires a colossal amount of administrative work and effort. Once the food aid juggernaut has been set on the road, it is tempting to let it proceed under its own momentum rather than make it change direction, or call it to a complete halt. For example, FFW schemes in Bangladesh began in 1975, just after the worst of the famine was over. Some 45,000 tonnes were sent in. By 1979, over 220,000 tonnes were still being distributed through FFW projects. As an AID report states, this five-fold increase took place in spite of the fact that food conditions had changed considerably between 1975 and 1979.

"Since [1975] there have been 4 consecutive years of good domestic food grain crops and an improvement in most economic indices. There is no famine and no massive starvation. The government has built up a food reserve of over 600,000 metric tons which can cover three to four months ration system offtakes." [59]

Nevertheless, the evaluator reported that the role of the FFW programme remained unchanged.

"[FFW] is still primarily a relief operation which is evaluated in terms of the amount of wheat distributed and the employment generated. Its longer term effect on rural poverty and development is paid little or no attention." [60]

And thirdly, as the case of Guatemala illustrates, there can be a great deal of pressure to continue distributing food, even in the face of local opposition. The reasons for this insistence are complicated — nervousness, inadequate communication with the field, a reluctance to believe that food aid could be doing any positive damage, etc. — together with the less honourable motives of convenient surplus disposal, competition with other donor governments or agencies or a chance to win public approbation by being seen to be giving assistance. Sometimes, there seems to be a kind of managerial inertia in which decisions are not taken. For example, the United Nations Relief and Works Agency for Palestine Refugees in the Near East (UNRWA) continues to provide the Palestinian refugees with regular rations of food aid. These began as a relief measure in 1948 and were resumed in 1967. A former UNRWA official states,

". . . . as a regular feature of refugee life food aid is a prime agent of the dependence relationship and the state of mind which it generates. In 1980, the number of refugees entitled to a regular ration issue was over 830,000. Although UNRWA recognises that the general distribution of food aid is no longer necessary, it has not terminated the programme." [61]

The onus must be on the donors to make clear from the start that foreign food aid is not to become a central component of subsequent projects, and to make a schedule for the steady reduction of rations, leading to their withdrawal as soon as possible.

How is Food Aid Released for Disaster Relief and Refugee Feeding?

Food aid for disaster relief from the US is released under PL 480 Title II and is handled principally by CARE, CRS and WFP. Much of the Title II food aid which goes straight to governments is also intended for this purpose. [62]

The EEC has a notorious record for the late arrival of relief food aid. The Court of Auditors of the EEC states, in its 1980 report, that it is "not acceptable that, on average, emergency aid should take three or four months to reach the port of unloading". [63] The Court further reported that it saw "emergency food aid (which took three months between the decision to grant aid and the arrival of the ship) still lying in store at the port of unloading two months later for lack, apparently, of available transport to the place of distribution". [64] It is hoped that 'triangular operations' will alleviate this problem; in 1979, food aid for Nicaragua, bought regionally, reached the country within a few days. (65)

In emergencies, the WFP can send food shipments at the discretion of the Director-General of FAO, on the recommendation of the Executive Director of WFP.

In spite of some streamlining of procedures for emergency food aid, the inadequate response of the donors to disasters has been the cause of some anxiety within the FAO and elsewhere. (66) In the first three months of 1981, there were appeals for over 4.8 million tons of emergency food aid. (67) Whether they are launched by the stricken country or are initiated on its behalf by the FAO, appeals may well be based on exaggerated estimates. Nonetheless, there is due cause for concern, since food has frequently failed to reach those needing it, in time and in sufficient quantities.

In 1975, in order to improve this state of affairs, the FAO set up the International Emergency Food Reserve (IEFR). This was to be made up of contributions of cash and commodities and placed at the disposal of WFP. But, in spite of frequent appeals to donor governments, the Director-General of the FAO told the European Parliament Development and Cooperation Group in 1980 that the Reserve "has never reached its target of 500,000 tons of grain" and that "in 1979, it barely exceeded 300,000 tons". (68) Moreover, of the contributions made in 1980, 13% was channelled bilaterally and over half of the donations were earmarked for specific emergencies, thereby reducing "the amount of the IEFR that is freely available for emergencies which may arise in any other country". (69) Thus, a WFP report states,

> "On the whole, only little more than a quarter (26 percent) of IEFR contributions in 1980 formally channelled through WFP could in fact be committed to emergencies in 1980. . . in a manner consistent with the envisaged concept of the Reserve. Even for those contributions, in most cases WFP had some delay in committing IEFR resources until donors confirmed the availability of the specific commodities required as well as their willingness to release their contributions for the emergency concerned." (70)

The report goes on to say that, as a result of these factors, "the actual modalities of the IEFR operations have departed from the original concept of a standby international arrangement to be used when and where necessary". (71) However, food is donated through alternative mechanisms. The report also notes that "in 1979 bilateral emergency food aid directly given by donors (other than through the IEFR) was about three and a half times all contributions to the Reserve". (72)

The problem is not, therefore, entirely one of availability; it is one of political choice. During 1979-80, political considerations about aid to Kampuchea meant that there were great delays in the commitment of food. The Non-Governmental Organisations (NGO) Consortium, led by OXFAM, felt that it was appropriate and necessary to make shipments of food and, being free from political constraints, was able to respond more quickly. Similarly, the recent official exclusion of Vietnam from access even to emergency relief for humanitarian purposes has meant that small agencies have again felt obliged to offer assistance in the form of food aid. (73)

There are proposals to make the contributions legally binding on the donors and freely at the disposal of WFP. (74) However, at the moment, the Director-General of the FAO has remarkable personal control over the IEFR (and other WFP emergency aid), allowing him in 1980 "at his own discretion – to dispose of emergency food aid amounting to a total value of US $200 million". (75) This has led to concern among some donors to WFP about the appropriateness of present decision-making and may partly explain why certain countries, the US and EEC in particular, have been unwilling to donate more than they do to the IEFR, or to have contributions to it made legally binding. (76)

However, the reasons for WFP's recommendations that donors should increase their **cash** rather than their commodity contributions to the IEFR, should be noted.

> "Moreover, experience has shown that it would be highly desirable to have a greater proportion of IEFR contributions in the form of cash for the purchase of commodities in the same regions as those affected by emergencies, thereby reducing costs and the time lag before the arrival of relief supplies." (77)

This echoes the EEC's policy on 'triangular operations' and certainly begs the question – if food can be purchased locally or regionally during emergencies, then it must also be available after the emergency is over and medium-term rehabilitation work has taken its place.

Conclusions

Food aid is often needed for emergency relief and this will often entail imports, especially for refugees.

It would be unrealistic to expect a fool-proof prescription for integrating food aid with disaster relief. However quickly assistance arrives, in certain types of disaster it is almost bound to be too late to avert suffering for some individuals.

Not all of the misfortunes associated with emergency food aid reflect badly on the donors. It is often difficult to determine the needs of the afflicted population or to judge the best time to make an intervention from outside. Potential recipient governments bear the major responsibility for making such decisions or for appealing for help when it is needed.

Nonetheless, in many respects, procedures for emergency food aid could be improved by the donors. Food requirements need to be assessed carefully and consignments of food made only if the commodities available answer these needs. At present, there are too few routine checks on donations to ensure that inappropriate foods are not sent. Also, potential donors should investigate within the stricken region or a neighbouring country to ensure that food needs could not be satisfied more swiftly and cheaply from local sources.

Food aid, if it is needed at all, must arrive at the right time. Donors need to find speedier ways of releasing food commodities once the need for them has been established. Conversely, they must recognise that prolonged donations may upset local recovery efforts and should, therefore, make firm plans to suspend supplies as soon as possible.

For the same reason, belated donations are, in most cases, unnecessary. Handling agencies need to be more flexible in their approach to distributing relief supplies, including food. Often, there is no need to give the food away and to do so may undermine the efforts of local farmers to market their own food, or of the local community to return to normality. Wherever possible, local people should select and participate in the distribution of food aid.

Donors should not use emergencies as a way of beginning long-term food aid projects. Once an emergency is over, food aid should be stopped.

3 FOOD FOR WORK

O f the different means of distributing food aid, food-for-work (FFW) is the most varied. It encompasses a number of approaches and methodologies, ranging from multi-million pound efforts to construct irrigation schemes and boost agricultural production to modest projects to stimulate local community development.

Of all the uses of project food aid, FFW is the only one which **has the potential** to increase local food production directly. However, the primary benefits of such programmes tend to go mainly to those who possess land.

TABLE I

LARGEST RECIPIENTS OF US FOOD AID THROUGHOUT FFW PROGRAMMES 1978 - 79. (1)

Total World Recipients 14,152,050

	Recipients	As Percentage of Population	As Percentage of Total Recipients
Asia (total recipients − 9,717,800)			
Bangladesh	7,168,500	8.1%	50.6%
India	2,023,600	3.1%	14.3%
Indonesia	234,500	0.2%	1.6%
Sub Sahara Africa (total recipients − 1,292,800)			
Lesotho	257,500	19.8%	1.8%
Tanzania	204,000	1.8%	1.1%
Somalia	137,000	3.6%	1.0%
Near East (total recipients − 1,195,900)			
Tunisia	239,700	3.9%	1.7%
Lebanon	215,700	9.9%	1.5%
Syria	154,000	5.7%	1.1%
Morocco	130,000	0.6%	1.0%
Egypt	123,100	0.3%	0.9%
Cyprus	100,000	16.0%	0.7%
Latin America (total recipients − 1,945,550)			
Bolivia	701,000	13.0%	4.9%
Peru	347,400	2.0%	2.4%
Chile	120,000	1.1%	0.8%
Haiti	119,500	2.4%	0.8%
Dominican Republic	93,700	1.8%	0.6%

This chapter will examine the impact on development of the three major types of FFW programmes:

Public Works,

Community Development and

Resettlement Projects.

Public Works

The principal aim in using food aid for public works is to provide labour intensive schemes in areas where there are high levels of underemployment and/or unemployment. A secondary objective is to improve rural infrastructure by building farm-to-market roads, introducing soil conservation measures, constructing irrigation canals and so on. It is hoped that such work might contribute to an increase in agricultural production. Public works projects have also included slum clearance, squatter settlement improvement, the erection of community buildings and even the salvaging of the Philae temples in Egypt. (2) In general, these programmes are run in conjunction with local governments' own development plans; in the case of WFP projects, local governments invariably make financial contributions to the work, often three or four times as much as the value of the food input. (3)

In accordance with the Protection of Wages Convention of the International Labour Office, WFP (with CARE the major sponsor of FFW/public works programmes) usually insists that workers receive at least half their wages in cash at the prevailing local rate and the remainder in food. (4) There are exceptions to this. In Bangladesh, where there are millions of people employed on FFW schemes, workers are paid entirely in food. (5)

The scale and physical achievements of FFW can be striking. The former Executive Director of WFP described his programme in Bangladesh as follows:

> "A four-year food-for-work programme which the Government has been able to undertake since 1975 with the help of 480,000 tons of wheat supplied by the Programme has already resulted in the clearing of nearly 2,000 miles of silted-up canals and the rehabilitation of about 3,000 miles of embankments. At times, more than two million men and women have been employed on this project, which is expected to increase the country's rice yield by 200,000 tons annually." (6)

The shifting of large quantities of earth to enable canals and flood embankments to be constructed makes up a large proportion of the work performed under FFW schemes (particularly in Bangladesh). Workers on this WFP project earned just over six pounds of wheat for every ton of earth moved. As a WFP booklet says, "on the larger sites hundreds, and sometimes thousands, of workers equipped with only hand digging tools and baskets large enough to carry 45 kg of earth at a time laboured from six o'clock in the morning to five in the afternoon, with a rest period at noon. It was calculated that with the use of these humble implements, more earth was moved by May 1976 than the total amount moved in digging the Panama Canal ". (7)

Food-for-work projects may provide employment for women and the old who would otherwise have difficulty getting jobs. The work is often hard, productivity is low and long-term benefits elusive.

When described in quantitative terms, such achievements are impressive. However, if public works are to be judged by the criterion of **development**, it is essential to consider long-term benefits. For unless the poor — those who work on the scheme — gain more than temporary employment, then the benefits in development terms are open to question.

Concern about FFW/public works focuses on three major points.

How good are the levels of productivity and maintenance?

How much real or lasting employment is actually created?

Do the projects serve the interests of the poor in the long term?

Maxwell, who conducted research for the survey of studies of food aid commissioned by the WFP, finds that there are "broadly two views" on the question of the distribution of benefits (assets).

". . . the first is that the assets are distributed in accordance with the existing pattern of ownership; the second, the majority view, is that public works actually tend to worsen the distribution of asset ownership. No study suggests that public works redistribute assets to the poor and this may be an important limitation of the approach, particularly since it is so often emphasised that workers must derive immediate benefit for public works to succeed." [8]

He finds also that the choice of many public works projects has "reflected inequitable land ownership" and thus worked in favour of the better-off.

"There are cases where small farmers and landless labourers do benefit from the asset creation of public works, but the weight of evidence seems to suggest that more often they do not benefit in proportion to their numbers." [9]

There is evidence from a number of countries that the long-term benefits go to those whom the projects are not designed to help rather than to those they are intended to support. The problem for the project planners is well defined in an FAO report on Tunisia.

". . . the WFP project cannot at present refuse any request for assistance even when this request comes from wealthy farmers who ask for the planting and maintenance of several dozen hectares: this amounts to a payment by the State, with WFP rations, of the wages of workers employed by the large proprietors and gives them the benefits of credits and subsidies intended in principle for the disadvantaged." [10]

In addition, land ownership patterns were made even more unjust by the establishment of plantations on what were collective lands; in Tunisia the planting of trees establishes a private claim to property and thus the project was likely to lead to the dispossession of the people who were working under the scheme.

By March, 1974, the programme had affected 60,000 families in 600 co-operatives. It had cost WFP $18 million and the Tunisian Government a further

$30 million. Fifty-five thousand hectares of trees and 90,000 hectares of forage crops had been planted. In 1979, an FAO expert engaged on the project wrote,

> "[This project] is a good example of the way in which aid, in principle intended to satisfy basic needs of poor rural people, in fact ends by increasing the economic power and control of land by the large growers." [11]

The Tunisian Government was not itself unaware of this fact, noting in a 1974 report,

> "At present, the food rations of the WFP project are given in proportion to the area planted, as are the payments for work-days on the irrigated area of Sbiba for vegetable and forage crops. **This favours the people owning the largest farms, those for which subsidies are least justified.**" [12] (emphasis added)

Stevens reports that in Botswana, the main beneficiaries in a "food for fallow" scheme also seemed to be the "larger more prosperous farmers". [13] And the World Bank reports a case in Ethiopia where workers on a reforestation project became disillusioned by the fact that the benefits were going to large landowners and so sabotaged it by planting all the trees upside down! [14]

By far the biggest FFW/public works programmes in the world are in Bangladesh. They began modestly as drought relief measurers in 1975 and since then have grown enormously and become virtually institutionalised. In 1979 there were 7.2 million participants (including dependents) enrolled on the US-sponsored programme alone (see Table I). There is growing concern about the whole effort and in particular the long-term benefits deriving from it. In 1979, a field worker living in Bangladesh was asked by an OXFAM-America official how FFW benefited the participants in the programme apart from by giving them food.

> "A. I don't think the work benefits them very much unless you think it's spiritually virtuous. The products of their work don't benefit them at all. The people who do the work are landless. They carry out improvements to land. . . . but the landless people don't own the land so they don't get any of the benefits. Now, theoretically, if you drain a piece of land, it becomes more productive and there might be a greater demand for labor, but it often doesn't work in practice.
>
> Q. If I were a landholder and the Food For Work program decided to improve my land by draining or leveling, do I then get free labor?
>
> A. You're absolutely right; that's how it works. That's a very important point which I think is generally missed. . . . What happens with Food For Work is that Union Councils . . . organise the distribution for Food For Work. . . So not only do they get the benefit of improving their land and their friends' land, but also

there's tremendous scope for using the power of patronage that it gives them. And also, of course, there's the possibility of diverting some of the resources without doing any work at all, which also happens to a large extent." (15)

Similar findings have come from AID and the Swedish International Development Authority (SIDA), among others. (16) In 1979, AID called for an evaluation of the secondary effects of FFW projects in Bangladesh, with reference mainly to the CARE programme. So many difficulties were encountered by the evaluator, especially with regard to the misappropriation of the food and to assessing just how much employment was created, that only a preliminary report was produced. Its conclusions are, therefore, tentative. It was found that where secondary benefits did exist they "unambiguously are biased in favor on the non-poor". (17) This leads to what is, perhaps, the report's major finding.

> "FFW results in increased inequity:— Since the secondary benefits of FFW mostly are related to the utilization of land few benefits will accrue to the landless. In addition to that the landless are losing a substantial part of the primary benefits. Seen over time it seems clear that FFW not only strengthens 'the exploitative semi-feudal system which now controls most aspects of the village life' (Akbar, 'Evaluation of Early Implementation Projects') but also speeds up the polarisation process in rural areas." (18)

The study gives several illustrations of how this happens. For example, a project to re-excavate a water tank (an artificial pond) ended in disqualifying those who had previously been entitled to use it. Earnings from the tank went to a single family and the general public was no longer allowed to use it even for washing or bathing.

> "It is difficult to identify any secondary effects of this tank project that are beneficial to the people in Sariakandi. Nothing has been produced from the tank during the two years since re-excavation. On the contrary there is a loss of production since some fish was caught prior to the re-excavation. Moreover the tank could previously be used by all local people, for bathing and washing whilst it now is a private tank. For the family in possession of the lease, it represents a potential extra income of 8 − 10,000 taka per year [approximately £250 − £300 at 1979 rates]." (19)

The report continues, "Comparing this tank with other tanks in Ishurdi it seems normal rather than unique". (20) Another tank had identical characteristics to the one already described. "[It] was poorly executed and left incomplete, is leased to a private person and no fish has [sic] been produced." (21) The largest tank in Sariakandi, re-excavated under a WFP—sponsored project, was much better constructed although no fish had been caught by the time this evaluation was carried out. It was expected to yield 4,000 pounds of fish per year starting in 1980. It was estimated that it would take 15 fishermen one week to harvest the fish, thereby creating 75 man-days of labour. A watchman was posted by the tank and the people who had restored it were prevented from fishing there. (22) An embankment project involving some 35,000 man-days of labour was benefiting people owning land in the area, including the chairman and several other Parishad (village committee) members. Extra income would be used to buy more land. However, landless people who depend on "agricultural labor and fishing for their living will probably have to face at least a temporary set back since they lose on fishing from the beginning and only in the future can benefit from increased employment in crop production." (23) Landless people who live entirely on fishing would from then on have to concentrate on river fishing, which is harder work and requires more equipment. Again, a road project led to an increase in land value of over 50% but "the largest beneficiaries are without doubt the farmers owning land in the flood protected area." (24)

There are even cases in Bangladesh of people losing their land through FFW projects, leaving them worse off than before. At times embankments and other works have to be constructed across land belonging to villagers. No compensation was given for the land used in the following case:

> "One of the villagers who owns a very small plot of land is very poor and the project passes through his land. Since the land utilized for FFW projects is contributed to the project on [a] voluntary basis, the poor villager received no compensation from the BDG [Bangladesh Government]. However, the PIC [Project Implementation Committee] gave this villager a few maunds [1 maund = 80 lbs] of wheat from the allotment on humanitarian grounds but the actual amount given is never recorded." (25)

This is not an isolated case in Bangladesh and reverses the proverb 'give a man a fish and you feed him for a day, teach him to fish and you'll feed him for life'. Here the man has his land taken away from him for ever and he is given some food to eat for a while.

It can thus be argued that in many cases the long-term benefits, where they exist, accrue to a relatively privileged group rather than to the poor and that at times, the poor are left worse off than they were before the project started.

Other factors further complicate the FFW/public works issue. Labour productivity and maintenance are generally poor, so that the projects deteriorate rapidly. Their contribution to development is therefore minimal. According to Stevens, a survey of the literature on FFW concludes that "productivity on most public works is abysmally low" and notes that "maintenance of completed assets is often so poor that very little benefit is derived." (26) He gives an example of FFW productivity in Lesotho which ranges from about four to eight times lower than cash-paid workers are expected to achieve.

> "What is particularly significant about these Lesotho figures is not so much that they are poor as that they may be considerably better than those in some other countries. Data on pro-

ductivity in Upper Volta are very rudimentary. However, the indications are that it is lower than in Lesotho, and may be only one-third as great . . . Even in Tunisia, where the government has considerably greater resources than exist in the other three countries, productivity . . . was very low." (27)

Furthermore,

"The experience of these four countries [Botswana, Lesotho, Tunisia and Upper Volta] is by no means untypical of labour intensive public works, whether or not they are food aided. Although a World Bank survey of 24 public works projects in 14 countries found that 'Tunisia appeared to have more than most (tasks) that could be classified as make-work . . .', it also reported many other instances of low productivity on low priority projects." (28)

The reasons for low productivity on FFW/public works range from the 'tokenism' of much of the work, the consequently low morale of the employees and the high proportion of workers who would otherwise be considered unemployable (ie, the old or disabled), to the fact that administration and supervision are often slacker than in conventional employment. Supervision of projects which involve the distribution of free gifts is itself difficult and since people are being paid in food (or a combination of food aid and cash), it is hard to insist on high standards of work. A supervisor can scarcely criticise someone for slow work when that person is being paid in free food aid. A WFP report comments:

"Although established in the Plan of Operations, no work norms are used in the conservation activities, and labour supervision is not always adequate in quantity and quality. The prevailing attitude appears to be that food-aid gangs work at no cost to anybody and therefore supervision is quite loose." (29)

The remarkably low standard of maintenance is sometimes due to the uncertain allocation of responsibilities. For example, in his evaluation of a ten year, $3,000,000, wells improvement project managed by CARE in Tunisia, a medical doctor found that after six years "more than 80 per cent of wells have pump failure. . . . with consequent pollution no different from that in unimproved wells." He continued: "CARE recognised from its own past experience and from that of others that maintenance was the key to providing continued potable water. Consequently, it formed and trained several mobile teams in the course of the projects, each team having been assigned to cover well and spring sites in specified areas." (30) However, an inspection of the wells in a defined area revealed that many of them were out of operation and that more than half the sample contained "highly polluted water as evidenced by the presence of large numbers of faecal coliform and/or faecal streptococci in the micro-biological analyses done." (31) In his concluding discussion, Dr. Wolfe observes,

"Poor countries never have enough funds for all their needs and well maintenance must be low on their list of priorities.

In much of the third world, it seems the attitudes towards wells is 'if the rich foreigners built them, it is their responsibility to maintain'." (32)

Another more basic reason for the lack of interest in maintenance is that it might actually be detrimental to sharecroppers' interests to improve land too much. For example, in 1979, the Inter-American Foundation reported a case in Haiti where peasant farmers participated in a FFW irrigation scheme, only to find that the landowners then increased the rent. (33)

Even if food aid were available to 'finance' long-term maintenance – a solution which challenges those who see it as an interim measure only – this crucial problem of land tenure would still remain unsolved, while the poor quality of much of the basic work would in many cases make maintenance impracticable.

The amount and type of employment generated by these public works depends on the individual project. Projects such as roads appear to provide more employment during the construction stage, in the short-term, while directly productive projects such as irrigation create more once they are in operation. Thus, some projects offer little long-term employment; even projects intended to increase food production may not provide much more. An AID evaluation report on Bangladesh gives one example.

> "Generally it is assumed that increased agricultural production leads to increased employment. The evaluation team has learned that this is not always the case. In some parts of Bangladesh a new irrigation canal will allow farmers to plant a *boro* crop which is high yielding and lower risk than the *aman* and *aus* crops he may have previously planted . . . He may experience some increase in production but the labor requirements of the *boro* crop are less than the combined *aman* and *aus* crops." (34)

Another AID report found that the amount of employment generated by FFW in Bangladesh was "systematically over estimated" (35) , with one method of estimating the total of work days giving a figure of 10.5 million, against CARE's own estimate of 22.7 million. (36)

Thus, the employment actually created may fall short of the claims that are made. In addition, the kind of work done can only be carried out in the dry season. In the case of Bangladesh, this climatic limitation means that FFW may overlap with periods when alternative employment opportunities are most likely to be available. (37)

There are, of course, more positive aspects of FFW/public works. A great many old, poor and unemployed people are enabled to take part in the schemes (38) and women are sometimes given the chance to participate in work usually reserved for men. At one time this was reported to be happening to a relatively high degree in Bangladesh, although the numbers were never very large and by 1979 were dwindling rather than increasing. (39) Some of the projects are of value to the community at large and employment is created in the short-term.

In spite of these 'welfare' aspects, however, the claims made for the FFW/ public works contribution to development usually fail to stand up to scrutiny. All too frequently people gain short-term benefits by participating in badly-designed schemes which certainly will not provide any long-term advantage and may even serve to undermine their position.

Community Development

In an article entitled "More calories, more protein, more progress", an AID magazine described this aspect of FFW as follows:

> "Many people lack food and many communities need work done on projects. This combination makes possible the Food for Work program. Under this program, Food for Peace Commodities are used as payment for services rendered on Community self-help projects." (40)

There is a certain overlap between public works and some community development projects – both include road building, for example – but in general the latter are small and are run at a more local level.

There are a few examples of excellent FFW-promoted community development work but there is concern about the motivation of groups which, with the offer of food aid as an incentive, form themselves to carry out projects.

In Haiti, community development is carried out mainly by '*conseils communautaires*' – community councils – which sound the ideal type of group to support. Unfortunately, as an AID report says, "Councils are often formed with a view to qualifying for food aid through work projects . . . Councils whose identity is linked to food aid tend to disappear when food aid is withdrawn." (41) They are known in Haiti as *konseys manjes*, or food councils. This somewhat 'cart-before-the-horse' pattern applies also to the work performed to justify the food aid. In 1978, a Caritas official described how the councils operate.

> "They construct roads in order to receive food . . . Where there is no more food, there can be no work. Goodbye food, goodbye road! If they got [sic] food in order to finish a road, they regret it as soon as they have finished the road. They only then wish for the deterioration of the road so that they can re-do it." (42)

This type of 'make-work' is found elsewhere and a similar analysis has been made by an AID official in the Dominican Republic. There, FFW has been much used for making roads. One agency supported the construction and repair of almost 7,800 miles of access roads in the six years between 1972 and 1978. (43) The official in an interview with the author commented that the voluntary agencies had rebuilt every secondary road in the country at least twice and every year had to rebuild them. He said it was "just an excuse to give out the food." (44)

This is by no means an isolated case. In Guatemala, after the 1976 earthquake, FFW caused problems, as a Mayan farmer explained. He needed help to harvest his crops but found difficulty getting it, partly because it was easier to do FFW work instead.

> ". . . they didn't have to do much in the 'Food-for-Work' program, just move around a little and they knew they would get their food in the afternoon. On the other hand, if you go to work in someone's fields, you have to work and it's hard work. While with 'Food-for-Work' it's mostly just a question of the person being there even if he doesn't do anything; but in the afternoon he gets his ration. . . If they did work [on the FFW project] they might be told to move some debris into piles or something like that. The main thing was to get through the day." (45)

In Lesotho a major programme of dam building to control erosion, road and airstrip construction and tree-planting was undertaken from the late 1960s in response to an emergency caused by drought. The author of a book on development in Lesotho found that,

> ". . . the vast majority of the trees planted were cut down by the Basuto or trampled by livestock long before they matured . . . almost none of the dams were built in the areas hardest hit by the drought, and . . . those that were built were scattered through the country without rhyme or reason." (46)

Few of the dams, he says, were used for any of the purposes for which they were intended. In one evaluation he read,

> "[The] CARE chief in Lesotho . . . noted that people tended to draw out the work to prolong their food wages, that most of the dams were used for watering livestock, if at all, and that they would have been ultimately cheaper to build with paid labor. However, [he] also felt that the program was justified because without food-for-work they would not have been built at all, and that part of the purpose of the program was to distribute food 'without the onus of charity'." (47)

This justification of inventing work to disguise the hand-out of food aid leads all too easily to the disappearance of the project. While this might avoid "the onus of charity", in the long run it might have two negative effects. The first is that communities are left with monuments to their own **incapacity** to help themselves. The second concerns a change in attitude and motivation on the part of the communities and individuals involved which can seriously undermine alternative approaches to development. The writer of the book on Lesotho goes on to describe the opinions of two Peace Crops volunteers about the dams.

> ". . . not only did the Basuto not know what the dams were for but the arrival of food-for-work dam projects had negative effects on nonwage community projects already in progress. One of them said, 'People would be working on a project for free, out of pride — gardens, water-supply systems and the like

– then the government would come in offering food to build a road or a dam, and everybody would abandon the community development project.' Both these men said that there was nothing self-help about the food-for-work projects because people only thought about the wages, and because they would abandon genuine self-help projects for the food." (48)

Similar problems were encountered by a team of field workers who visited the north west of Haiti in March 1978. A doctor reported to them what happened when a FFW project to help build contour canals was started. "All the center's work with motivation was destroyed, and now that community will do nothing without FFW." In another town the local development co-ordinator told the team that FFW was an integral part of the programme "although agents said that FFW ruins people." (49) The report ends by noting that "Everyone realised the detrimental effect that FFW has had on community action in the NW. . ." (50) A 1975 FAO report on the community development aspect of FFW in Haiti says that,

". . . attempts to involve some of the surplus labor in FFW aid projects have extremely deleterious effects on the peasant communities and cause great erosion of the reservoir of mutual service relationships of the traditional peasantry." (51)

A person who had worked for a number of years with two agencies which use food aid in Haiti described how the very mention of food aid can cause dissension within community groups.

"In the Central Plateau, an agricultural agent even had to make representations to a CARE official to get him not to intervene in the region. People were accustomed to meeting and discussing their problems. Just one meeting with this person, who promised food aid, was enough to bring out differences in the group. Each person wanted to be in charge of distribution, and to achieve that, began to criticise his neighbour." (52)

The problems caused by food aid and the fact that good results are obtainable without it are illustrated in this extract from a 1980 OXFAM report on a forestry and agriculture project in West Africa:

"The project director observed that the use of food aid as an incentive to farmers to participate in community development work has distorted their conception of the value, long and short term, of the work, and has concomitantly undermined the interest that a farmer usually has in the future of his community. Often, among farmers who have received food aid in the past for participation in community development projects, the overriding concern is with food aid. . . .

No food aid was offered to farmers participating in the project and as a result, instead of revolving around food aid and its distribution, the project spent its energy and time working with farmers interested in the immediate and future well-being of their community. To a small project these two interests — food aid and rural community development — are mutually exclusive. Interest in one precludes a genuine interest in the other." (53)

The project director found that the solution was

> "to work with farmers whose interest is not in receiving food for their work, but rather in improving their farms and their village with their work. Farmers with this latter interest, in their community rather than in food aid, pursued their work on run-off systems and are already having productive results from their labors." (54)

The AID report on Haiti mentioned previously also comments on this aspect of FFW — its tendency to focus attention on the food itself rather than on independent progress that might otherwise be made.

> ". . . the food for work focus of many councils tends to divert attention away from the serious business of grass roots peasant organisation and economic alternatives." (55)

A corollary of the motivation issue is the lack of maintenance which is as much a problem with community development projects here as with FFW/public works. In Haiti there is a phrase to describe what happens when the food aid stops, 'Food [sic] suspendu, travail suspendu' — 'no more food, no more work'. (56) Stevens likewise reports that one criticism made about the FFW road building and improvement scheme in Lesotho "is that villagers now refuse to maintain their roads without further food aid". (57)

As with public works, the choice of project is crucial and may affect the quality of work performed. In Haiti, the emphasis on road-building has more to do with the desire to distribute food aid than with the pursuit of well-planned development aims; as in Lesotho, the onus of charity is avoided but at the cost of 'make-work, or worse. The AID study on Haiti describes how, according to food agency staff, on the island of La Gonave, "roadwork constitutes a convenient method for readily assembling large numbers of workers and distributing considerable quantities of food". (58) This aspect of FFW, the report says, "has generally had the effect of fostering long term work projects which drag on and are somehow never completed. Roads, for example, include false starts or traces which are later determined to be inadequate and recharted along other paths, effectively extending the work project". (59) Thus on the island, 300 km of jeep roads have been constructed although "there is no commercial vehicular traffic of any kind". Local people tend to go on foot, and goods are transported by boats or beasts of burden. Almost the only vehicles to use the FFW road system were those of the food agency staff, Protestant pastors and the occasional private motorcycle. (60)

All the above signs suggest that the projects are determined more by the pressure to distribute food aid than by an objective appraisal of the needs and priorities of the local community.

It is possible that community-based FFW may actually worsen the lot of the peasant farmer. A group of US volunteers surveyed one area of Haiti to discover who had worked on a scheme to introduce soil conservation techniques. There were 129 households which reported members who had been involved in the work. The survey reported that FFW workers had been obliged to work on community leaders' land for one day a week during the harvest and for four other days on other projects. Workers were left little time to tend their own gardens and "were relying on the food received from CARE or more honestly, on the money obtained when that food was sold". [61] The report concludes,

> "It is the opinion of volunteers working in the area that the soil conservation project has been a detriment to the development of the area. . . FFW has hurt the initiative of local farmers. The project was also used by local community leaders to oppress the rural peasants." [62]

Alternatively, there are examples of FFW stimulating or strengthening community development programmes. This has sometimes been the case in the Dominican Republic [63] and in certain Indian projects, where an AID report cites cases in which "the food served as a starting point for a process of developing a sense that people could exercise control over their own lives." [64]

One of the most striking of these cases is the Kottar Social Service Society in Southern India, where food aid from CRS is used. Exceptionally good project management has built on favourable local conditions — such as a high level of formal education amongst the population as well as more equitable land-holding patterns.

> "The Kottar experience illustrates a beneficial use of food aid. The food is targeted to nutritionally 'vulnerable' groups . . . It is also linked to community organization and mobilization behind an impressive range of self-help efforts." [65]

The author of the report concludes by explaining why this is an "isolated success story".

> "Alas, if the 'ingredients of success' are easy to identify, they are very difficult to replicate. Simply to list them is to reveal how rare they are individually, much less all together . . . The Kottar Social Service Society and what it represents are more the exception than the rule. If Kottar impresses us, we may have to accept the fact that, as a model for emulation, it is not transferable. The overall effect of considering the Kottar experience is sobering rather than exhilarating." [66]

Whilst it may be that community development projects generally have to settle for less than these standards of excellence, there are factors mentioned in an AID/India report which are important for any responsible development project. In contrasting the "best projects" with those FFW schemes which "appeared to generate an attitude of utter reliance on help given from outside the community", the evaluators identified three crucial characteristics; the "involvement of [the] recipients at an early stage, the requirement that recipients contribute their own resources and labor, and the provision for continuation of the project after the termination of food donations". (67)

An OXFAM field officer involved in a FFW scheme in India in 1981 identified local control and organisation of the programme as the one indispensable characteristic of a valid food-aided project.

"... this is so far the best and most beneficial programme for the poor and the poorest in the rural areas **provided the planning and execution is exclusively left to the organisation of the poor** ... The FFW programme can **also** [sic] impoverish people rather than helping them if proper safe-guards are not taken up." (emphasis added)

Resettlement Projects

The arguments in favour of FFW can be most persuasively made in the case of resettlement projects. People who are being resettled on unused or reclaimed land may face food shortages in the first few years, before their crops have been established. Food aid is provided to tide them over this period and to support the construction of irrigation canals, schools and health clinics. The kind of work undertaken is, therefore, similar to both public works and community development.

The 1978 Food For Peace Annual Report describes a project in Morocco, where considerable land improvement is being undertaken.

"The government is providing the materials, equipment, and engineering skills. AID is providing Title II commodities and a grant of $100,000; CRS is managing the program. The people of Figuig are providing the volunteer manpower. These community volunteers will receive Title II food on a self-help basis during construction, and will share in the use of the reclaimed land that will be divided among the farmers and herders living in the project area. Some 13,000 people inhabiting these marginal areas on a subsistence economy will directly benefit from the project." (68)

The WFP goes further and argues that the benefits of resettlement projects are not merely physical.

"In the course of the development work, these new settlers will have been inculcated with ideas of service to the community and are therefore all the more ready to cooperate with others in ensuring the success of the new settlement." (69)

Since settlers should soon be able to fend for themselves, society at large will also benefit.

"These people will therefore cease to be a burden on the national economy as underemployed and undernourished workers and can look forward — provided they are willing to work and to learn — to a better future for themselves and their families." (70)

However, there are problems associated with resettlement projects which cannot be addressed by food aid as such — principally who makes the decisions governing resettlement and whether the people want to be moved. It is not unknown for governments to move people against their will.

The other major problem is encouraging self-sufficiency at the earliest possible date in order to ensure that food distribution is not institutionalised. This can be difficult, as this case from a Somali project illustrates:

> "They [the WFP mission] felt that it should, however, be made clear to the Government that, after eight years of WFP aid, there would be little possibility of further WFP aid after 1983, even if the project objectives of self-sufficiency in income/food production had not been achieved by that time." (71)

Conclusions

Obviously, food aid can never hope to be very much more than a social palliative, since it cannot itself address the causes of poverty or unemployment. However, there is much evidence that food aid has been used with inadequate awareness of the detrimental consequences that FFW projects can have on the people who participate in them. Truly successful FFW schemes — those in which the participants benefit **after** the actual work is over — are the exception rather than the rule; in the majority of cases, there is little or no improvement in the living and working conditions of the poor.

Too frequently, people on FFW/public works projects are exploited as free labour for those who are already relatively well-off. In many cases, the extremely low levels of productivity indicate that the projects are providing 'make-work' rather than furthering long-term development.

Whilst the provision of undemanding employment for those who might otherwise by considered unemployable — the old and disabled, for example — may be commendable in itself, it should not be confused with development. It is welfare.

The products of FFW schemes frequently deteriorate and the development benefits — whether in practical or less tangible terms — are therefore questionable. Where lasting benefits are produced, they are often irrelevant and sometimes harmful to the poor who helped to create them.

As far as FFW/community development is concerned, the fact that local people are by definition more likely to be involved in the planning is to some extent a safeguard against the kind of misdirection of benefits associated with FFW/public works. Nonetheless, there are two areas of caution:

1) it needs to be openly recognised that the very offer of food aid may determine the motivation of the community leaders or otherwise compromise the direction of projects, and

2) the risk of creating or encouraging projects which are dependent on foreign food aid is a real one, to be avoided at all costs.

In some cases, FFW projects have been initiated more to satisfy the desire to distribute food than in response to a clear idea of how the work performed will contribute to development. The AID report on India puts this explicitly.

> "Repeatedly in interviews with project holders, we were told that requests for projects were never refused except in the cases of deliberate malfeasance. The US AID Food for Peace Officer acknowledged that projects were often allocated without adherence to a criterion of economic need, and justified this by the difficulty of finding viable projects . . ." [72]

This chapter has not claimed that FFW cannot succeed under any circumstances. Rather, it has argued that the necessary conditions exist only rarely, and that to intoduce food aid into projects which are not viable or cannot handle it properly has been shown to be positively detrimental to the poor and to development work in general.

Child health clinics which concentrate on the distribution of food aid foster the idea that foreign food is more desirable than local products. Food handouts detract from nutrition education.

4 MOTHER—CHILD HEALTH PROGRAMMES

FOOD AID AND MOTHER-CHILD HEALTH PROGRAMMES

The biggest international effort to combat malnutrition in children is food-aided supplementary feeding for pregnant women, nursing mothers and children in the vulnerable under-five age group (hereafter referred to as MCH*). In 1978-79 there were over 16 million participants, using US food aid alone. [1] MCH programmes are conducted principally by voluntary agencies and WFP, often in conjunction with local governments. MCH programmes accounted for 33% of US project food aid in financial terms in 1978-79 but for only 24% of recipients. [2] Thus, MCH programmes are relatively expensive to operate.

MCH programmes — through feeding centres and health clinics — distribute food aid either in a ready-prepared form to be consumed at the centre, or as rations to be taken home. Nutrition education is meant to constitute an important part of these programmes. In theory, the children receive additional food while their mothers learn how to feed their families better; the children's nutritional condition improves and mothers are taught how to guard against subsequent relapse. Thus, MCH programmes are supposed to combine short-term relief feeding with long-term development through preventive education.

However, according to evaluations of the impact of MCH, practical results do not follow so smoothly. Far from ensuring nutritional improvement and acting as a means to promote health education over a longer period of time, this use of food aid is unable to guarantee the former and tends to encourage the very attitudes that run counter to long-term self-reliance.

Supplementary Feeding and Nutritional Improvement

The assumption that supplementary feeding will make a significant impact on malnutrition is challenged by the findings of project evaluators and field workers. In 1980, the CRS Medical Director for Sub-Sahara Africa reviewed his fifteen years' experience with food-aid nutrition programmes and noted:

> "The question is: Does supplementary feeding, added to education and the development process, provide the answer to the [nutrition] problem? One would like to say Yes, but experience, and extensive literature on the subject, tells us that the answer is No." [3]

A 1977 CARE report on its feeding programme in five countries — Colombia, Costa Rica, Dominican Republic, India (Tamil Nadu) and Pakistan — compared weight for height, height for age and weight for age of children participating for less than five months, more than nine months and a control of non-participants.

*Other health programmes, not using food aid, are often also called MCH. In this chapter MCH refers only to programmes using food aid.

"Few differences", says the report, "in nutritional status among the various groups within each country are large enough to be significant on any of the measures . . ." (4) The AID doctor in the Dominican Republic commented that the findings "suggest that the CARE program is having little effect on the prevalence of malnutrition among children being fed". (5) An AID-funded evaluation of MCH in Honduras found no particular difference between those children who were and those who were not receiving the supplement. (6) Caritas in Guatemala was unable to find any significant differences between children who had been receiving food aid there for over 18 months and those who had not. (7) A nutritionist surveyed two villages in Ghana: in one, a 'modernised' village, food aid was given to pre-school children, while in the other, a remote and more traditional village, there was no such programme. The levels of malnutrition in children were found to be similar in both places, with 50% of them suffering from mild malnutrition. (8) These findings were confirmed when the nutritionist began a family health programme in twelve villages. Again she found as much malnutrition in villages that had received supplementary food for three and a half years as in those that had never received any. (9) The biggest MCH programme in the world is in India. In 1978-79 it had over 8 million participants. (10) A 1980 evaluation of it for the US Government, referring to MCH as "massive supplementation programs", states:

> "Nutritional status does not seem to have improved, not even for those who have received the Title II MCH ration more or less regularly. The assumption that food aid could be 'targeted' like a rifle shot at nutritionally vulnerable groups around the world and therefore would improve their nutritional status has not been supported in spite of the transfer of millions of tons of food and herculean efforts by the volags [voluntary agencies] to ensure its proper use." (11)

The report concludes that,

> ". . . the major objectives of Title II food in MCH programs, that of improving health and nutritional status of the target group are largely not achieved. . . This finding is confirmed by much of the research done by Indian institutions, which failed in most cases to find any but marginal nutritional impact of MCH programs." (12)

A study of MCH in Morocco, conducted in 1979 for AID, drew the following conclusion:

> "In the context of the group of children who are intended beneficiaries of the MCH *Centres Sociaux Educatifs* project, MCH rations probably help children in normal nutritional status and good general health to maintain that state, but do little to improve the nutritional status of children suffering from moderate malnutrition, and have no effect on severely malnourished children." (13)

Thus, the major beneficiaries were those children already in relatively good health; and since they were well nourished before the programme began, it does not follow that they needed food aid. A subsequent AID report on the CRS-sponsored MCH programme in Morocco did find significant nutritional improvement due to the large size of the ration and effective nutrition education. However, 68% of the children were not malnourished to begin with. (14)

MCH programmes have sometimes had detrimental effects on participants. A survey in the Dominican Republic, found that food aid was encouraging malnutrition. Pre-school children were weighed monthly for two years. All were malnourished and ate a ration at an MCH centre. The children did not noticeably gain weight except during the mango and avocado seasons and whenever food aid **stopped**. After questioning the mothers, the nutritionist concluded that when children received food aid, mothers tended to over estimate the value of this foreign 'wonder food' and so fed them less local food. Whenever the food aid failed to arrive, mothers would, as a matter of course, ensure that their children had food, since they would never leave them unfed. This resulted in a weight gain. The experiment was repeated elsewhere and the findings were confirmed — with food aid there was no weight gain; without food aid weight increased. (15)

Even where nutritional improvement has been noted, it may not last long and children may simply regress to their former state of malnutrition once they leave the programme. In the Philippines, where some improvement was found, AID found that the "small amount of data gathered to assess [the long-term effect on nutritional status]. . . do not suggest that program graduates continue to progress nutritionally, or even hold their own, once graduated from the program". (16) In addition, many children in the vulnerable 6-11 month age group became worse off during the feeding programme and the evaluators recommended that,

> **"CRS should mount a special investigative effort to determine why such a large proportion of their 6-11 month olds regressed in nutrition status (59%).** CRS discovered this problem in the course of one of its own evaluations and has indicated to the team that they do intend to investigate. This should be done fairly soon, since the basic objective of bringing normal and mild 6-11 month olds into the program is to prevent malnutrition." (17)

Displacement or 'leakage' of the ration is one of the major reasons why supplementary feeding has not produced significant nutritional improvement. Though the child's intake of food is meant to be increased by the amount of the supplement, in practice this is impossible to guarantee. If the ration is eaten at the centre, then the child may be given less to eat at home. If the food is taken home, there is nothing to stop its being shared with other members of the family. Either way, the ration becomes, in part, a substitute for local food and not a supplement to it. The implications for local agriculture will be examined in Chapter 8 but substitution itself defeats the object of **supplementary** feeding programmes. A former UNRWA official has reported:

> "Even that part of the food aid programme that UNRWA has

traditionally believed to be particularly valuable, the EEC-funded supplementary feeding programme. . . is of doubtful value. Experience elsewhere in the world suggests that supplementary feeding quickly turns into substitutional feeding, the recipients of programmes simply getting less food at home. In fact, evidence is growing that groups which do not receive supplementary feeding usually enjoy the same nutritional status as those of the same community who do; and UNRWA's experience seems, at first glance, to be consistent with this evidence. In 1978, a WHO report on the health needs of Palestinian refugee children concluded that 'the growth and development of the refugee children in east Jordan can be taken to be not different from that of the general population in that country and consequently the marked improvement in the refugee children (since a previous study in 1963) is also seen among non-refugee children' (i.e. children who do not receive supplementary feeding)." (18)

An AID health sector assessment for the Dominican Republic calls attention to the gap between the theory and the practice.

"Supplementary feeding programs are justified as being an intervention that can provide immediate but temporary food supplements to 'at risk' recipients until such a time that they are no longer considered malnourished. It is the hope that by providing food while offering some nutrition education, the recipients will not be permanently dependent on the supplementary feeding programs. However, the operation of the PL 480 Title II program in the Dominican Republic has in practice become centered around food replacement rather than food supplement." (19)

Since substitution is an important factor determining the high failure rate of MCH in nutritional terms, some evaluators have suggested that increasing the rations may be a way of overcoming the problem. The five-country CARE report states:

"The primary explanation of why many children hadn't eaten the ration in take-home feeding was that the mothers had run out of food ahead of schedule due to sharing the child's ration with the entire family . . . Rations need to be increased in take-home feeding to assure that the supplies are not exhausted ahead of schedule, and that the intended child gets fed an adequate quantity." (20)

However, there are arguments which challenge the validity of this solution. In 1980, the Medical Director for CRS in the Sub-Sahara recognised the social consequences of increasing food aid.

"In fact, there are limits to the amount of food aid you can give a family for the child. These limits are set primarily by the administrative costs and by other considerations such as sale and exchange of food commodities and disincentives to local production." (21)

To increase rations of food aid may also have little impact. An evaluation of the PL 480 feeding programme in Honduras states:

> "Gain in weight (or weight loss) of 93 children was obtained at one day care centre covering a period of 8 months. Even though they were being fed **three meals and snacks**, only 51% of the children met the standard increase in weight. . . . On the other hand, 43% of the children lost weight during the 8-month period." (22) (emphasis added)

The lack of positive results may also be due to the foods used in MCH programmes. "Most of the PL 480 foods available for distribution are soy-fortified, high protein foods." (23) Although suitable for medical interventions in cases of severe malnutrition or protein-deficiency, these foods are no longer recommended in cases of slight malnutrition, where the immediate need is for a high calorie intake. ". . . . where basic calories are deficient, many of the artificial protein-enriched foods that are distributed are simply an expensive means of providing calories." (24)

Targeting Food Aid Through MCH

Ensuring that food aid is precisely 'targeted' to those mothers and children most in need is, as noted above, extremely difficult. In fact in many projects little effort is made to do so. Criteria for selecting candidates for feeding programmes are frequently lax or even non-existent. An AID draft report on the Dominican Republic comments:

> "At present, in all three agencies, a needy person is one who goes to a distribution center and expresses the need to be included in a program (MCH or FFW)." (25)

In 1979, US Government evaluators in Tanzania noted:

> "Weight, height, and age criteria for determining eligibility for MCH food were often not followed in Tanzania. Frequently, any child brought to the center was fed." (26)

The five-country CARE report emphasised this same point:

> ". . . the feeding programs enrol many children who are not malnourished. This is primarily because no criteria are used to target any of the programs to only the malnourished." (27)

In Upper Volta, Stevens observed that the majority of a sample population surveyed had an acceptable weight on their first visit to the MCH centre, while in Lesotho, "except among present attenders in the mountains, the number of new entrants with an unacceptable body weight never exceeds 27 per cent of those attending". (28) In other words, almost 3,000 of the 4,000 children need not have been attending the centre. Stevens concludes that "the findings of the

CARE report are confirmed: many beneficiaries of supplementary feeding are not malnourished at all". (29)

The AID-funded evaluation of the programme in India draws the same conclusions.

> "We also observed that in many cases children were given food supplementation on a first come first served basis rather than being screened for participation on the basis of nutritional need." (30)

The 1979 evaluation for AID of the programme in Morocco underlines the point.

> "No attempt to examine nutrition status enters into the selection of individual project participants, for example, or into the general allocation of Title II commodities among provinces." (31)

The question of the best age at which to enrol children on the programme was noted in the five-country CARE report which observed that on-site feeding programmes "are less likely to reach the most vulnerable younger preschooler because of the difficulty of transporting the young toddler to the center daily". (32) In 1972, an assessment for the US Government found that,

> "A major problem of nutritional impact remains, which is whether the MCH activities. . . . . are really reaching the weaning child between the ages of six and 36 months. . . Helfenbein, in his nine-country study for CARE, expresses similar doubts. David Call of Cornell Graduate School of Nutrition, who has extensively studied nutrition intervention. . . . feels that this most vulnerable sector of the most vulnerable group is not being reached to any significant degree in current Title II MCH efforts." (33)

One of the main recommendations made in this study was that,

> "The age range of child beneficiaries under the maternal/child health guidelines should be lowered to six months through three years, rather than the 0-5 year guideline. . . This measure should assure improved nutritional impact on those truly most vulnerable." (34)

Seven years later, in 1979, the evaluation conducted for the US Government in India concluded that "it should be recognised that few children under three years are being reached by the program". (35) This is especially significant when it is realized that in 1979 MCH projects in India being run by CARE and CRS (those projects under review) accounted for over 6.5 million recipients, i.e., 40% of all MCH participants receiving US food aid. (36)

However, the main criticisms directed at the value of supplementary feeding do not concern the age group of the recipients or whether or not there is a consequent improvement in health. The **real** discussion about the validity of MCH should centre on whether it is a suitable solution to the problem of malnutrition in the long term. Even if MCH had a positive effect on health, other factors should be taken into account which still make it a highly questionable approach. These include the cost in cash and staff time (see Chapter 6) and the fact that the distribution of free foreign food is an inherent contradiction to the nutrition education part of the programme.

Nutrition Education

Nutrition education is the principal means by which MCH programmes are intended to contribute to development and to ensure that recipients do not become dependent upon the supplements of donated food. The 1978 Annual Report from the Food for Peace Office of the US Government states:

> "In the developing countries food assistance provided through Title II. . . . in many instances has been the difference between death or mere existence and improved nutrition and health. However, feeding programs alone are insufficient as needy peoples must also be helped. . . . to become self-sustaining through increased food production and nutritional knowledge necessary to put the food to its best uses. Title II. . . . is dedicated to alleviating the problem of chronic hunger . . . . through supplementary feeding programs while providing nutritional education. . . ." [37]

Similarly, an AID statement on food aid to the Dominican Republic says:

> "Where feasible, gardens are attached to the [MCH] centers and maintained by the mothers who share the produce. Where gardens are not practicable the nutrition lessons — an integral part of the feeding programs — include information on nutritious foods which can be grown at home." [38]

In practice, the education component has usually been found wanting. A CWS/Dominican Republic report states that the MCH centres are "merely feeding centers". [39] Other field reports tell a similar story. For example, the five-country CARE report says:

> "Nearly all the centers visited in the present survey claim to be providing nutrition education to the mothers. However, little evidence of nutrition education was observed except in Colombia where nutrition education is an integral component of the feeding program. . . Almost none of the centers visited were measuring children. Therefore growth charts were not being used to monitor the progress of beneficiaries nor to educate mothers regarding the nutritional status of their children." [40]

The evaluation done for AID of MCH in Honduras reported that,

> "Educational activities are supposed to be required for each of these centers. However, no education activity was observed in the visits made by the field team to different centers." [41]

The 1975 Annual Report from the Food for Peace Office relates how, in India, the US voluntary agencies, together with the Government, were collaborating in "mass nutrition education" (42) , yet in 1979, it was estimated that over 60% of the MCH programme under review in India amounted simply to food distribution, with no other services being supplied, while of the remaining 40%, less than one-quarter provided "some educational activities". (43) (emphasis added) Therefore, only a small percentage of the total programme was giving more than "occasional health and nutritional classes". (44)

The common response to such findings is that nutrition education should be incorporated into MCH programmes. The evaluation on India recommends that "programs which provide food alone should be upgraded to provide other health and educational services". (45) This solution pays no attention either to the **reasons** for the general lack of educational services, or to the difficulties in providing them. For example, the additional expense that such "up-grading" would entail − both financially and administratively − might well be prohibitive. To provide real health services for the 4,000,000 people registered on the India programme and who are not currently receiving them is a colossal challenge.

However, there is evidence to suggest that to hand out free foreign food as an incentive for health or nutrition education runs counter to long-term development goals. It has been observed, in a number of countries, that mothers tend to go to health centres for the food rather than for the related services. Thus, motivation to attend may not necessarily outlive the provision of food.

- An evaluation undertaken in Ethiopia found that ". . . women coming to the distribution centers are paramountly concerned about the food they are going to receive and take nutrition education as one of the administrative constraints they have to go through to get food". (46)
- An AID survey in Guatemala reports that "at many Health Posts, people will come in for treatment of a preventive kind only when there is food available". (47)
- In the Gambia, attendance of mothers at a CRS clinic dropped from 40 to 10 when it stopped distributing oil and gave away only rice. (48)
- A WFP report from Pakistan states that "Provision of food appears to attract beneficiaries as could be seen from statistics available in some centres showing a drop in attendance when the project was interrupted". (49)

Just as on large programmes it is impossible to prevent food supplements being used as substitutes, so the idea of using food aid as an incentive to attract women to listen to nutrition classes is hard to put into practice. The donors' desire to provide classes is a stronger motive than the recipients' wish to attend them. It is not always clear what the education component is intended to achieve or how it is of practical relevance to the beneficiaries. As a means of encouraging changes in food habits it has not met with marked success. For example, CARE has conducted research to find acceptable and effective ways of promoting nutrition information and communicating the need for modest changes in local feeding habits.

"Messages included were (1) introduction of solid foods into the infant's diet after 6 months, and (2) introduction and/or increased consumption of green leafy vegetables by pregnant women. Two approaches were used: a positive, persuasive approach was used in half the test area, while the other half was exposed to a negative, shocking, fear-related approach... After the campaign, a survey was conducted to evaluate the message's impact. The shock approach was more successful than the positive one and had better retention. . . . . The campaign increased awareness, but it did not change people's food habits — this was especially true in the case of introducing solid foods by 6 months." [50]

The five-country CARE report also found that "more mothers knew the cause of malnutrition than what they could do to treat it". [51] Likewise, a report submitted to the UN states that "sufficient documentation does exist to conclude that often little behaviour change occurs even in the face of high awareness." [52]

In the course of preparing a United Nations International Children's Emergency Fund (UNICEF) document on MCH, its authors reviewed over 200 reports on such programmes throughout the world. They found that where education did exist, it was "usually directed toward appropriate usage and targeting of the distributed foods". [53] For example, a WFP evaluation of the MCH programme in Bangladesh states that, "mother's receptivity of the nutrition message and of the advice given for the proper utilisation of the WFP ration appears to be very good". [54] This is instruction for short-term needs rather than nutrition education for long-term development. The advice does not equip the recipients for the day when food aid stops. This exemplifies the contradiction implicit in the aim to encourage independence by means of imported food aid. The AID health sector assessment for the Dominican Republic noted,

"First, the foodstuffs used in the PL 480 Title II program are not available in the local market. Therefore, educating mothers in their use tends to create a permanent dependence upon these imported items." [55]

Three experienced field workers in Guatemala likewise question the message inherent in the use of imported food.

"Nutrition programs based on free foreign food convince many mothers that their children can only be healthy if they consume the foods given away in the program. Often these foods are not available or would be prohibitively expensive if the family were to try to buy the same thing locally." [56]

Well-documented cases of the use of baby foods in countries where conditions are far from ideal, reveal the effects of attitudes like these. Not only are these foods expensive, but it is impossible to ensure that women (many of whom are illiterate) understand or follow the instructions on the packet, or that they can guarantee the necessary sanitary conditions for the safe use of these artificial foodstuffs. (57) A nurse who worked for two years in the OXFAM-funded Lake Kenyatta Settlement Scheme in Kenya made the following observations:

> "The distribution of dried milk runs into . . . problems. By distributing milk in the CRS program, whatever we say in talks about the dangers of not breast feeding we are unwittingly condoning bottle feeding . . . [The mother] would be better off to supplement the child's diet with eggs, locally grown pulses and vegetables — which would be greater in quantity, and cheaper. However, to bottle feed is becoming a status symbol . . ." (58)

An OXFAM field worker in North Yemen has described how a long-term medical programme was undermined by food handouts.

> "Two days a week this particular centre became a food distribution point rather than a health centre. It was completely disrupted . . . there is **no** education associated with food distribution. Handouts quickly degenerate into a farce and physical chaos, with hordes of women milling around trying to get the food. And entirely the wrong ideas on nutrition are encouraged. For four days a week, mothers are told not to waste their money on infant formula and are encouraged to breast-feed instead. You want this advice to be credible, and then you spend the days handing out imported food. It just doesn't make sense. Also, food aid promotes the belief that development comes from the outside, and that foreign foods are nutritionally preferable . . . in fact, they're often not even appropriate, and certainly less so than foods locally available, of which there is no shortage. . ." (59)

A major problem is that health centres frequently serve as food aid dispensaries. An evaluation of a nutrition education programme in Ethiopia attributed its weakness in part to "the fact that it is mainly given at food distribution centers". (60) This point was amplified:

> "The general population seems to look [at] the activity of the NFW (Nutrition Field Workers) [as] restricted to distribution of relief foods only. Regarding nutrition education, the understanding of the people is that NFW's presence is to give instructions on ways of getting relief foods and no more." (61)

Sometimes, the availability of food aid undermines work already in progress. A doctor working in Indonesia has written that an extensive nutrition project in East Java, which started in 1979 had, after a year, been "generally recognised" as a failure. This was attributed to "the presence of the food supplement . . . . unfortunately the addition of PL 480 and other foods have totally diverted the educational component, the basic purpose of the project, to one where village people line up to receive free food". (62) Comparable problems are demonstrated in a report from a field worker in Togo.

> "We had a good group of women in Togo studying nutrition in one village, but they heard that in another village about 10-15 kms away, a group of women receiving similar classes were also receiving free milk powder. They suspected they were supposed to receive the same stuff, so a lot of women quit coming to the classes because they thought they'd been cheated." (63)

An OXFAM Field Director in Africa experienced similar difficulties. Relief food aid was distributed in clinics where educational and vaccination programmes had been working satisfactorily.

> "Enormous damage can be done to on-going MCH programmes by the sudden requirement to distribute free food. Clinic attendances soared for the wrong reasons, some clinics turned into virtual battle-grounds, and the benefits of steady educational and vaccination programmes were lost." (64)

The original field report on which this conclusion was based illustrates another problem with free distribution programmes in general — the risk of encouraging self-centred behaviour rather than community-minded attitudes.

> "(The health team) have an average presence of 300+ at the clinics at present and are having trouble coping because they are dishing out free food from the WFP/EEC etc. They are fed up with the whole hand-out scene. Not only is it wrecking their clinics, but it's changing the attitude of people towards the Mission. Anyone who thinks the population are standing gratefully in line to receive their rations is sadly mistaken. 'Give it to us — it's ours' is rather the cry and not a helping hand is offered to load or unload the trucks. It's pretty soul-destroying for everybody!" (65)

Such changes in attitude have been noted by field workers elsewhere. A Caritas report written in 1979 for a parish in Guatemala suggested that "given the difficulties and quarrels that food distribution generates, dependency it creates and resignation it produces. . .", it should be discontinued at MCH centres. (66) One of the reasons for the decision to stop food distribution at some centres in the Philippines was that it was "often a cause of quarrels and disunity". (67)

In fact, alternative measures for improving health care are frequently devised when the distribution of food is suspended or decreased.

- MCH centres in one area of the Dominican Republic stopped distributing food aid because, according to a survey, it was encouraging malnutrition. Instead, emphasis was placed on teaching mothers how to grow their own vegetables, improve hygiene and prepare better balanced meals. This was a practical way of promoting nutrition and a direct approach to education. A survey conducted in 1978 showed that in a sample of over 5,000 children, an additional 22% had

51

reached 'normal' nutritional status during the four years following the cessation of food aid distribution. There had also been a drop of 5% in the number of children with mild malnutrition (from 49 to 44%); of 10% in those with moderate malnutrition (from 22 to 12%); and of 3.25% in those with severe malnutrition (from 4 to 0.75%). The positive trend in nutritional terms was significant. Haemoglobin levels also showed a marked improvement. Special recuperation centres were set up for the treatment of severely malnourished children. A key feature of these was teaching mothers how to keep their children in good health after leaving the centre. In about 95% of the cases, this was achieved. More important in development terms, brothers and sisters also showed some improvement without their receiving special care or food aid. This indicates that the education had been effective in the short-term and had been retained and applied over a long period of time. Not only was this done without food distribution but the closing of the feeding centres was the first and possibly essential step towards achieving such results. (68)

— A project in Nepal stopped the distribution of powdered milk and CSM (Corn-Soy Milk) and began to make more use of locally available food in its work. The clinic staff found that, once relieved of food distribution duties, they were able to spend more time with mothers in their homes and could thus learn from them about their problems and devote more time to encouraging them how best to use the food they already had. (69)

— Malnutrition rates in one area of Ghana are reported to have dropped substantially through an organised health programme involving only local foods. (70)

— In Jamaica, where Government policy in the early 1970s promoted self-reliance in food, a nutritionist found that when food prices in St. James' Parish almost doubled and food aid was cut back by two-thirds, malnutrition levels in rural areas decreased as people were encouraged to grow and eat more of their own food. "What did in fact happen from 1973 to 1975 was not an increase in malnutrition in St. James, but a **decrease**. In the rural areas the nutritional status of children improved significantly. Serious forms of malnutrition . . . . decreased by 50 percent from 9.5 percent to 4.5 percent . . . Urban rates remained about 4 percent with no significant deterioration." (71)

These examples demonstrate that it is possible to improve the effectiveness of MCH centres without relying on food aid and suggest that free food distribution may inhibit local initiatives to devise more suitable approaches to the problems.

Nevertheless, according to the authors of the UNICEF report on supplementary feeding, there may be advantages enjoyed by the participants in MCH which are not adequately measured at present.

"We remain unconvinced that either the true effects or the full benefits of food distribution programs have really been measured in the reported studies. Unless our current concepts of physiology, our current estimates of energy requirements, or our current approaches to the estimation of need in the individual and the population are seriously in error, the existing programs must be having effects that are not measured in terms of such parameters as body size and morbidity/mortality changes. We have argued in our report that another outcome, measured in only one of the studies we reviewed, may be voluntary activity (including play in children) and that this may affect psycho-social development and family/community interactions." (72).

However, the unintended disadvantages of MCH programmes must be included in evaluating their effectiveness. It would be perverse to insist that such indefinable benefits as 'voluntary activity' and 'play in children' should in themselves justify the continuation of programmes which fail to achieve their primary and tangible objectives.

Apart from calls for increasing the quantities of the food, better monitoring of programmes and wide-ranging evaluations of their impact, the only new suggestion to date for improving MCH comes from the CRS Medical Director for Sub-Sahara Africa who puts forward the idea of a "contractual food assistance program".

"A contractual food assistance program works like this: The parents of the child are made aware that the increased family revenue represented by the foods entails certain added reponsibilities and obligations which are satisfied by submitting themselves to an educational program and by upgrading the feeding and the general care of the child." (73)

The major difference between this and existing approaches to supplementary feeding is that here it is proposed that,

"When failure [to demonstrate satisfactory growth in the child] is due to a default in utilizing the increased revenue for the betterment of the child, as it happens when the foods are sold, exchanged or used as a sheer substitution of the traditional diet, you apply suitable and acceptable measures aimed at re-inforcing the agreed on obligations." (74)

Whether this would prove any more practicable than the current methods is a matter for speculation.

The purpose of channelling large inputs of food aid through the MCH system is to improve the nutritional status of the recipients. At present, emphasis is still placed on why MCH has failed to guarantee these improvements and on ways in which the programme can be made more effective in short-term nutritional respects.

Comments from three different reports help to highlight the inherent problems of MCH programmes which call their usefulness into question whether or not there is an improvement in nutrition levels. The first is from a letter written by a priest in the Philippines, explaining why, after almost six years, it had been decided to discontinue food distribution through MCH.

> "It cannot be denied, that from the beginning the TMCHP [Targeted Maternal and Child Health Program] could not really be seen as the most ideal approach to development. The distribution of food commodities, aside of being not too effective in the fight against malnutrition, has been experienced in these past few years as a factor that creates dependency rather than self-reliance. It may be functional as a temporary emergency help, but in the long run it becomes rather an obstacle than a stimulance to development." (75)

Secondly, an AID paper states:

> "To attack the nutrition problem piecemeal and ad hoc is to tinker with the machinery without making any really significant improvement in nutrition and in health. To have programs that 'do good' does not necessarily achieve significant and lasting results. Impact can be beneficial in some respects without really coming to grips with the problem, providing thereby only an illusion of progress." (76)

Thirdly, Maxwell, in his study of the nutritional impact of food aid, partly based on research carried out for WFP, concludes:

> "First, existing supplementary feeding reaches only a very small proportion of the priority target group. Second, supplementary feeding has in practice proved largely ineffective in nutritional terms. Third, even where it has been nutritionally effective supplementary feeding has not proved to be cost-effective. Fourth, small non-nutritional benefits may be balanced by non-nutritional costs. It would seem that a more frontal attack on poverty is needed. But what if such an attack is not forthcoming? Can supplementary feeding then be a way for international agencies to provide a palliative? [The evidence suggests] that the answer to this question is 'no'." (77)

In conclusion, MCH should be considered as a feeding rather than a nutrition activity. A summary of findings from a variety of reports emphasises that,

— MCH has generally had little effect on malnutrition.
— Many children in the programme are not malnourished to begin with.
— Significantly, the most vulnerable 1-3 age group is not being reached.
— Millions of recipients, especially in India, are merely getting food handouts. To classify them as MCH participants is to describe them incorrectly.

- Very often there is no nutrition education given.
- Education linked to food distribution is usually instruction in how to use the food aid – it is not nutrition education.
- Where nutrition education is taking place, the distribution of food aid tends to work against the nutrition message – food distribution and nutrition education are generally incompatible.
- The continued emphasis on protein-fortified foods has not kept pace with nutritional findings over the last 20 years. Protein-fortified supplementary feeding is largely irrelevant except in cases of severe malnutrition.
- The costs in cash and staff time are high, higher than those of alternative strategies which have proved successful.

The case might yet be made for a carefully targeted and monitored programme to treat severely malnourished children. This might be carried out in Nutrition Recuperation Centres (NRCs).

> "It appears that NRCs are very effective in accelerating growth rates and recuperating third-degree malnourished children . . . . NRCs . . . . are specially geared and distinctively equipped to meet the particular needs of the severely malnourished, who must be attended to. Furthermore, the percentage of third-degree malnourished children in the population is relatively small; thus the higher per-child costs still can be managed within total government budgetary constraints." [78]

This chapter has aimed to show that there is much misunderstanding about the objectives and achievements of MCH feeding. By trying to feed the millions, programmes fail to reach many severely malnourished children. As a 1980 UNICEF report says,

> "Undoubtedly . . . many segments of the population which are in real need of additional food are not being reached by existing programmes, and perhaps could not be reached by programmes structured as they are." [79]

Nothing could more clearly underline the need for programmes such as these to be revised and redirected.

In developing countries it is the better off families that can afford the luxury of sending their children to school. Very poor children, who would benefit most from additional food, must work to help support their families.

5 SCHOOL AND OTHER INSTITUTIONAL FEEDING

nstitutional feeding, principally through schools, is a major means by which food aid is distributed. In 1978-79, 18.4 million children were receiving US food aid in the form of school lunches. (1) Thus, school feeding reaches more people than the US-sponsored MCH programme, that is, 28% of all recipients of US project food aid. (2) In many countries, such as Egypt, Upper Volta, India, the Philippines, Sri Lanka and Haiti, school feeding is the largest project food aid programme sponsored by the US. (3) Supplementary feeding is meant to improve the nutritional status of the beneficiaries and to act as an incentive to children to attend school. Most of it is distributed through primary schools although WFP has expanded its work to include secondary schools, universities and colleges.

> "Food aid to schools, universities and training institutions helps to improve proficiency and regularity of attendance, reduces the dropout rate and increases the range of candidates for entry. Simultaneously, it improves their state of nutrition and helps to promote good dietary habits. Furthermore, as a result of WFP assistance, funds previously used for food can be released for investment in the expansion of existing education and training facilities or the creation of new ones." (4)

Donor agencies also provide food aid to other institutions such as day-care centres, orphanages, old people's homes and hospitals. In a study of US voluntary aid, John Sommer says of these institutional programmes:

> "They are concerned with long-term relief (more properly described as welfare) in the sense that people confined to such institutions would not have the necessary sustenance of life without such aid, and that in most cases the institutions are unlikely to ever become self-supporting." (5)

According to figures for 1978-79, recipients in such institutions accounted for only 2% of the total number of recipients of US project food aid. (6)

School feeding appears to be a convenient way of operating a food aid programme — the distribution network and the target group already exist. However, it is important to consider the nature of the target group — the children who go to school. In many countries, compulsory education is purely nominal; there is usually a large discrepancy between the attendance rates of children from urban and of those from rural areas, and girls' education is frequently taken less seriously than that of their male contemporaries.

Stevens reports that of the four countries he studied (Tunisia, Lesotho,

Botswana and Upper Volta), the highest rate of enrolment was achieved by Tunisia, with 70-75% of the primary school age population attending school. In Upper Volta, only 10% attended. But these figures conceal important regional variations, which mirror differences in relative affluence. The richer coastal governorates of Tunisia had an attendance rate of about 75%, whereas the poorer interior had a figure of 57%. "Similarly, in Upper Volta the low national figure conceals an even lower 4 per cent for the Sahel *département* in the extreme north of the country." [7] In Botswana, pupils tended to come from richer households. Stevens concludes that,

> ". . . . even if all schools were covered, the lunch programme would still miss substantial sections of the population, and there is every reason to believe that those children who do not attend school are more vulnerable than those who do . . . .
>
> This would not necessarily be a major criticism if at least the school population contained a substantial proportion of poorer people even if it excluded the poorest. . . . However, there is some evidence that the lunch programme does not simply miss the poorest groups, but positively discriminates against them because primary school children come from essentially non-vulnerable backgrounds." [8]

Reports from other countries verify Stevens' conclusion. The biggest US school feeding programme is in India, where there are over 9,000,000 recipients. [9] Nevertheless, a 1979 US Government investigation states that in India, "AID has often noted that children from the lowest strata often do not attend school". [10] The same report adds that in Sri Lanka "the school feeding program has become overextended and is feeding a lot of children who really are not that needy. . ." [11] Thus, school feeding contains, in many countries, what Stevens calls a "built-in bias" against the poor. [12]

If children receiving food aid are often not the **financially** vulnerable, it is important to ask whether they are the most **nutritionally** vulnerable. At the start of its 1981 Food Crusade, the Executive Director of CARE stated:

> "As little as $5 provides 600 nutritious biscuits to school children. Only $15 supplies a nourishing bowl of porridge for 300 school children for a week, and often this supplemental food makes a significant difference in a child's health and survival as well as learning ability." [13]

However, children of **pre-school** age are the most nutritionally vulnerable. A WFP report on a school feeding programme in Brazil involving 229,000 recipients, notes this aspect. "It is said that those at the age of school entry suffer in their studies from their poor nutritional status on entry. This suggests that greater emphasis should be placed on pre-school feeding for younger children." [14] Moreover, school feeding does not provide children with food throughout the year; most feeding takes place only when classes are in progress — usually for no more than five days a week and only during those months when school is in session. Indeed, in Brazil, meals are provided for only 144 days a year.

". . . . the nutritional improvement brought about by the WFP supplement was found by the mission to be minimal. This is due to the rather small fraction of the year (much less than half) in which the children are receiving the food, and to the small quantities of food on average reaching each child on those days when there is feeding (less than 200 calories per day, or less that 10 percent of daily requirements)." (15)

The nutritional impact of supplementary feeding has been examined in the discussion of MCH programmes in Chapter 4. The same conclusion – that any actual impact is generally slight – may be made for school feeding. Indeed, supplementary feeding in schools may so interfere with the children's normal diet that they do better during school vacation when the supplement is unavailable. An AID draft report on food aid in the Philippines, for the period 1970-80, concludes its analysis of the nutritional impact of school feeding as follows:

"**Analysis of the data from nine schools in Ilocos Sur, the Bicol and Manila revealed that during the 1st year of program participation no statistically significant change occurred in the nutrition status of Grade I – Grade IV beneficiaries.** Of the nine schools, two revealed a statistically significant increase in nutritional status (Pin Yahan (CRS) and B.P. Ragasa (CARE)), two other schools showed a statistically significant decline, and five schools revealed no change. . .

The analysis revealed no consistent trends in nutritional status during the months of school vacation that would suggest that the program is having a maintenance effect. . . beneficiaries of three of the schools in the Bicol were better off during the school vacation when program participation came to an end . . . . What were the nutritional trends of the children when they returned to school during the following year? **The analysis revealed no statistically significant change in nutrition status of beneficiaries during the second year of program participation** . . . For one school, it was possible to obtain longitudinal data for a four year period. . . **The analysis revealed no statistically significant change in nutrition status of beneficaries participating in the program over a four year time period. . .**"
(16) (original emphasis)

Of all the schools studied, only one showed a statistically significant nutritional improvement over a two year period and this was one in the control group where no food aid was distributed. (17)

One writer notes that in India, ". . . . all too often the target groups do not benefit much; children fed at school often receive correspondingly less to eat at home, or take the food home where it is divided among the family". (18) An analyst who studied food aid projects for the FAO in nine countries, made a similar observation in Senegal, calling it a "fact of apparently world-wide validity". (19)

The argument for school feeding, however, does not rest solely on its nutritional impact but on the incentive it is assumed to provide for pupils to attend school and the education benefits this will bring. There is some evidence of a positive impact on school attendance as a result of supplementary feeding. Maxwell reports that,

> "The evidence on this question is largely qualitative but two studies in India by Prodipto Roy have found evidence of a 5-10% increase in attendance, especially in the lower classes of primary schools and among tribal children. The studies were not able to find any impact on performance, though one study at a school with a well organized programme, in Coimbatore, India, did find significant improvements in mental ability and behavioural characteristics." (20)

According to WFP, primary school enrolment in Mauritania in the years from 1967 to 1979 (while school feeding was in progress) increased in a "spectacular" manner from 10.3% to an estimated 23%. (21)

The 1979 evaluation done for AID in India also found that the impact of school feeding on attendance was satisfactory.

> "From numerous visits and inquiries the team has concluded that the main objective and the main benefit of the MDM [mid-day meal] program is the role of the food as an incentive to the child himself and to his parents for his attendance at school. Everyone — GOI [Government of India] and local officials, CARE personnel, teachers and parents — was unanimous on this point." (22)

However, the 1980 AID assessment of the educational impact of school feeding in India questioned the extent of these improvements. For example, in the State of Madhya Pradesh, ". . . . it took approximately seven months of participation in the program to increase school attendance by a single day". (23) The investigation concluded,

> ". . . . . the evidence . . . . . lends little support for a strong relationship between increasing school attendance and the presence of the school feeding program. Thus, while the program appears to have increased attendance rates, reduced absentee rates, and stabilized the month-to-month variation in attendance and enrolment, particularly among the lower primary grades, these impacts, even though significant, are extremely small." (24)

Other reports do not identify a significant increase in school attendance during the provision of the food supplement. The WFP/Brazil report found that "It does not seem that the provision of food had a very strong influence in increasing school attendance".(25) There are a number of contributory factors. First, there is the rate of absenteeism, ". . . one cause being the calls upon older children to help their poor parents either at home or by going out to earn". (26)

Second, there is the problem of pupils repeating a year, ". . . . about half of the children have to remain in the same grade for a repeated year, particularly in the lower grades". (27) Third, absenteeism and repeating can lead to pupils dropping out entirely from the school system. These problems are common to many countries, despite the fact that school feeding is widespread.

— "In Africa between 10 and 46 per cent of pupils repeat their first year in primary school, in Latin America between 18 and 35 per cent. The final year of primary school . . . is the favourite for repetition. Between 20 and 54 per cent of African pupils repeat primary grade 6. . ." (28)

— In 1971, AID reported that in the Dominican Republic, of 800,000 children enrolled in primary school nearly 70% were in the first three classes. It was estimated that only 17% of them would complete their primary education, while in rural areas the figure would be 7%. (29)

— In Haiti in 1977, only four out of every 100 who started primary school completed it successfully. (30)

— In Guatemala only 4% of rural children and 50% of urban children complete their primary education. (31)

— In four Latin American countries studied by the United Nations Educational Scientific and Cultural Organisation (UNESCO) the average success rate for completing primary school was 50% for urban and 20% for rural children. (32)

— In Egypt where a high proportion of children attend school, only 53% of primary school age children in 1973 reached the final year. (33)

— The AID/India report quotes the primary school drop-out rate as 60%. (34)

Given the above figures, the aim of using school feeding as a means to improve attendance and performance in those children who go to school seems more ambitious than might at first appear.

Practical difficulties arise if the school feeding system is not stable enough to act as a reliable distribution mechanism. The smooth running of the programme depends upon a host of imponderables, any one of which can seriously disrupt the project. The 1981 WFP/Brazil report illustrates just how intractible such problems can be.

"Within the average [amount of food eaten] there are considerable variations, far in excess of what is an acceptable deviation, due to practical difficulties, in the amount and in the type of the food commodities reaching each child.

In some schools, second helpings were not permitted. The main reason was that the kitchen facilities, including the size of cooking utensils, were inadequate to permit cooking of greater quantities, or even to provide each child with a full plate at the first helping. In quite a number of schools the children have to bring their own plate or receptacle, so that the amount they eat, in the absence of a second helping, depends on the size of their receptacle." (35)

In the Central African Republic, a school feeding project was hampered by the "dire lack of communication between the central project office and the provinces which, compounded with the irregular supplies of commodities, [led] to gross deviations from project modalities and misinterpretations of project objectives". (36) At the macro-level, these problems included irregular supplies, "deficient operating accounts" and "substantial losses" due to the combined effects of pilfering, damage, insect infestation and unauthorised sales. (37) At the micro-level, the problems were also severe, although the project had been in existence for 5 years.

"The mission observed in most canteens visited that the limited food available was distributed to all or a majority of children and students on a rotating basis by dividing them in five groups, each receiving a meal once a week. This of course is not only contrary to the principle of selection, with a result that the needy students are deprived of daily meals, but it provides no basis for achieving the project objectives, whether educational or nutritional. . . . It is hardly necessary to add that, when in operation, the canteens usually serve only WFP commodities without supplementary local food, and there is no attempt to observe the WFP-prescribed rations." (38)

A school feeding programme of 14 years' standing in Botswana also experienced operational difficulties.

"School kitchens could be better designed so that they cause less smoke; many cooks, even in schools with new kitchens, still prefer to prepare the food outside, unless it is raining. The few schools that are without kitchens do not have food on wet days. Cooks should be taught to conserve wood, brought by the pupils, by not cooking blended food for a long time, as is the custom with traditional porridges." (39)

In an account of a WFP programme in Senegal, the author states that,

"Although the school year started in October, none of the canteens was yet functioning at the beginning of November. Theoretically, the number of meals served was to be five per week, but we found that three out of six canteens provided only four meals a week. On a surprise visit, we found that five out of six of the schools in our sample served no lunch at all, although there was no serious reason why the canteens were not functioning." (40)

Conclusions

Children who receive regular meals at school in addition to those they normally get at home clearly benefit from this form of supplementary feeding. However, it should be recognised that in many developing countries, this particular method of distribution tends to be biased against the poor, who are less likely to attend school and who are more likely to leave prematurely. In addition, operational difficulties mean that often there is no satisfactorily-organised school feeding in progress.

Possibly, the provision of school meals does act as an incentive to start school. However, any success is undercut by the high drop-out rates that still occur. (The figures given in this chapter refer only to primary schools; the secondary school population is even smaller.) In addition, management of this food has proved difficult, especially in Africa. [41] If the aim is to encourage poor children to study, it might make better sense to pay for their school fees rather than to provide food aid to those who are already able to attend.

Unlike school feeding, welfare feeding through other institutions is uncomplicated. It does not attempt to turn food aid into development but to do what only **food** can do — feed people in need. Yet, this uncomplicated welfare feeding accounts for only an insignificant proportion of total project food aid.

The problems described in this chapter illustrate the fact that in practice, school feeding programmes are unable to transcend the limitations of the system through which they operate. The ready-made distribution mechanism that is assumed to be an advantage in fact is structurally incapable of reaching the poor.

The practicalities of distributing food aid rations can take up time development workers could use better. Community workers and health personnel are expected to take responsibility for measuring out rations and keeping records, when they should be concentrating on the jobs they were trained for.

6 THE COST OF PROJECT FOOD AID

*A*pproximately £500,000,000 is spent each year on project food aid. Although the food is **donated**, it has to be **bought** by donor governments at commercial prices. In 1979, the cost — including processing — to the US Government of Title II food aid was $393,000,000. (1) An additional cost is sea-freight, which, in 1979, came to over $209,000,000, or 53% of the value of the food. (2)

Once it has been delivered to the recipient country, there are further costs, including warehousing and internal transport, and the food requires considerable administration at every stage. In 1976, the **total** running costs of the US food aid programme in Guatemala were conservatively estimated at 89% of the cost of the food itself (Table II).

Not all of these costs are borne by the donors. Once US food aid is in the recipient country, US handling agencies usually take over transport and distribution. In many cases, recipient governments will offset the agencies' administrative costs, both in the country and the US. For example, CARE-India is reported to have 'repatriated' to the US over $1,100,000 from the Indian Government for the period 1979-80. (3) In 1979 the combined contribution to one agency alone from the Indian Government and States was $41,000,000 (Table III).

WFP pays for the food to be transported to the port of unloading and sometimes makes a contribution towards internal transport costs, particularly in the least developed countries. However, the recipient government is always expected to share financial responsibility for projects; often its contribution outweighs by several times the value of the food input. (4) The EEC in the majority of cases contributes to transport and distribution costs. (5)

The associated costs of project food aid are, therefore, high in relation to the amount of food donated. Costs are also subject to annual increases, largely due to inflation. Thus in 1978, it cost the US Government $328,000,000 to buy 1.67 million tonnes of Title II commoditiies and in the following year it cost $393,000,000 to buy only 1.46 million tonnes; this represents an increase per tonne of 37%. (6) Costs for sea-freight increased even more. In 1978, they represented 40% of the value of the food; the following year this had gone up to 53%. (7) This trend has been reported by WFP, which announced that "ocean transport costs increased by 13% during 1980" and that administrative costs went up by 15%. (8) In presenting these figures the Executive Director of WFP commented:

> "In the light of strong inflationary trends, it seems evident
> that expenditure on these items will continue to rise in 1981
> and subsequent years." (9)

TABLE II: ESTIMATED NON-FOOD COSTS ASSOCIATED WITH PL480/GUATEMALA PROGRAMME*

1.	**SEA FREIGHT**	Shipment from USA to Guatemalan ports paid by Government of the United States.	35.0%
2.	**INLAND TRANSPORT**	Guatemalan ports to inland, regional distribution points; minimum $350,000 cash paid by Guatemalan Government.	4.0%
3.	**FOOD MANAGEMENT**	Warehousing, distribution, management and other costs (reported by CARE and CRS as having combined value of $3.2 million per year in cash and in-kind contributions).	45.0%
4.	**LOSSES**	(a) **Marine** (during ocean transport). Exact costs are unknown; this % is an *estimate* only of normal marine insurance rates.	0.3%
		(b) **Commodity Condemnation** (based on the 1,000/tons of maize declared unfit for human consumption by Guatemalan Government in 1976, taken as a percentage of the overall 1976 programme).	4.0%
		(c) **During customs and inland transport.**	0.4%
		(d) **Spoilage** at inland points.**	0.3%
		OVERHEADS of US Dept. of Agriculture, of Dept. of State, through AID, Washington and Guatemala, and of CRS and CARE New York, cannot be estimated but probably represent a substantial amount of additional investment.	
			89.0% in addition to the cost of the food

* Note: Based on 1977 figures; cash costs are converted to percentages of food costs. These figures are *estimates*.

** AID advises this may go as high as 25%; thus, the total percentage - 89% - is probably too conservative.

FROM: Jo Froman et al., *General Review: PL480 Food Assistance in Guatemala*, Antigua, Guatemala, June 1977, p. 17.

Recipient countries do not remain immune from the consequences of inflation in donor countries. For example, the Dominican Republic received over $94,000,000 of US project food aid between 1962 and 1978. (10) The Government of the Dominican Republic provided free warehousing for the food and also contributed over $13,000,000 to the distributing agencies, principally to support supplementary feeding programmes. (11) Also, to offset freight and distribution costs, beneficiaries of projects made contributions of money officially estimated, for 1973-74, at $550,000. (12) Substantial costs accumulated over the period, owing to the use of trained personnel, such as health workers and teachers, to distribute food aid. By 1977, as a result of inflation, the Governments both of the US and the Dominican Republic were paying considerably more for much less food aid.

"In 1969/70, 30,000 tons of food aid cost $7.5m, and the Dominican Republic Government contributed an estimated $868,000.

In 1976/77, 23,000 tons cost $9.65m, and the Dominican Republic Government contributed $1.2m." (13)

The high costs of the food aid approach to development might be justifiable if the projects achieved their objectives. However, as has been shown,very often projects are unsuccessful and even when they do achieve their aims, the approach is very expensive.

Maxwell quotes a report which found that in India it cost half as much again to prevent a child's death through supplementary feeding as it would by providing basic medical services, and that "for children aged 1-3 years, nutrition supplementation was up to 11 times more expensive in terms of lives saved than medical services". (14) Maxwell concludes that "even where it has been nutritionally effective supplementary feeding has not proved to be cost-effective". (15) Since supplementary feeding programmes involve so many people who are **not** malnourished, costs are much higher than they would be if projects were effectively targeted. When factors inhibiting the efficiency of the programme were taken into account, it was calculated that the recuperation of one child in an MCH nutrition centre in Guatemala would cost S2,671. (16) The five-country CARE report referred to in Chapter 4 estimated that the costs of non-targeted MCH programmes may be up to **ten times** greater than those of projects which concentrate on feeding malnourished people. (17) It concluded:

"Unless ways are found to target programs to more malnourished children, to reduce the number of family members sharing the ration, to reduce substitution, and to increase the number of children eating the ration daily, it is doubtful that feeding programs can be a cost effective means of reducing the rates of malnutrition amongst preschoolers in developing countries." (18)

The report quotes the cost per head of supplementary feeding for malnourished children in the Dominican Republic as $66-$74 a year. (19) As noted in Chapter 4 this programme has little nutritional impact. Thus costs recur as children return year after year to the programme and other members of their families are also enrolled. The emphasis on distributing food rather than on prevention evidently provides no solution here.

By comparison a smaller nutrition project in the same country has had good results. This treats carefully identified malnourished children at recuperation centres. It costs $100 a child for the three-month recuperation period, on the surface a relatively high figure. However, **no** food aid is used in this project (except for a little Dutch milk powder), and the emphasis is on intensive health education concentrating on locally available foods. In this case about 95% of the children remain well-nourished after leaving the centre and their brothers and sisters also improve. [20]

School feeding programmes are also badly targeted for combating malnutrition in the very poor or the nutritionally vulnerable. The school feeding programme in India accounts for over half the world total of participants in such projects. [21] However, a recent AID evaluation states:

> "The evidence on the feeding program's impacts on measures of school efficiency such as improved attendance, reduced attrition, and better academic performance is, at worst, meager and inconclusive. At best, it suggests that the program has had a minimal impact on its principal objectives, which, if compared to the costs of the program, represents an extremely ineffective and inefficient use of scarce resources." [22]

The evaluator points out that in India "the average state government in 1978/79 spent Rs.164 per student to educate a child in primary school. Compared to this, an expenditure of Rs.60 per year to feed a child in the Mid Day Meal Program was sizeable, equivalent to over one-third the amount of educational resources expended on that child". [23] He concludes:

> "While it may be argued that the food or commodity component would not be converted into funds to increase expenditures on primary education, this food is not a free good. It does have other uses. . ." [24]

In FFW projects, cost-effectiveness in development terms will ultimately depend on whether they provide **long-term** benefits to the people who helped to build them. One of the conclusions of an AID report of FFW in Bangladesh is that the marketing effects of FFW road projects were "negligible and hardly feasible to measure" because the roads deteriorated too quickly to permit any changes in marketing practices. [25] In the absence of proper maintenance, many of the works constructed through FFW lost their effectiveness after two to three years. [26]

In such cases, the cost of implementing a programme may exceed the value of the benefits it produces. Stevens reports a large-scale FFW project in Botswana where "the value of the public works created did not offset the cost of the project; indeed, it would have been cheaper for the government to have handed out the food aid free of charge than it was to make people work for it". [27] Even excluding the costs of the food aid, transport and government personnel,

TABLE III: STATE GOVERNMENTS AND GOVERNMENT OF INDIA INPUTS INTO CARE, SCHOOL FEEDING AND MCH PROGRAMMES[1]
(Value in 1979 Dollars)

| | State Governments | | | | Government of India | | | Total (States and Govt. of India) | |
| | School Feeding | | Pre-school (MCH) | | | | | | |
	Indigenous Food Inputs (2)	Personnel and Overheads (3)	Indigenous Food Inputs (2)	Personnel and Overheads (3)	Balahar (4)	Personnel and Overheads (3)	Cash Grants	Indigenous Food Inputs (2)	Personnel and Overheads (3)
1976	8,872,153	7,042,409	5,217,267	7,120,661	1,925,000	–	–	16,014,420	14,163,070
1977	9,654,275	8,601,768	5,609,025	7,062,562	2,750,000	–	–	18,013,300	15,664,330
1978	15,069,880	10,482,146	10,585,250	17,054,445	2,865,000	750,000	3,078,600	28,520,125	31,365,125
1979	20,897,740	14,865,027	15,861,020	18,337,226	2,865,000	932,500	6,913,377	40,352,510	41,053,130

(1) CARE Fiscal Year 80 Programme Plan.
(2) Indigenous Food Inputs refers to direct purchases of local foods to supplement Title II food inputs.
(3) Personnel and Overheads refers to logistical support in terms of transport, storage and personnel.
(4) Balahar is an indigenous food product manufactured using 85% Title II food and 15% indigenous food
The values shown here are those of the Government of India's indigenous inputs.

From: *An Evaluation Report of the P.L. 480 Title II program in India,*
Community Systems Foundation, Ann Arbor, Michigan, 4 June, 1979, p.24.

the project cost about $30,000 more than it was worth ". . . in terms of the value of works produced". (28)

The opportunity cost of food aid is also high. The food alone requires considerable administration in both donor and recipient countries. Often, recipient governments have to provide personnel as well as cash to support the distribution. The potential waste is especially high with skilled people such as nurses, doctors and teachers, obliged to devote attention to routine distribution of food. For example, a general review of nutrition rehabilitation centres found that "much more attention by staff is given to feeding and caring for centre children than to education of their mothers. . ." (29) A WFP report on a $19,000,000 feeding programme in the Pakistan notes that distribution "appears to be rather time consuming for lady health visitors (nurses) and other staff". (30) A WFP evaluation of a large school feeding programme in the Philippines found that food distribution had "substantially increased the workload of the teachers. . . In order to implement the project activities satisfactorily, some sacrifices have to be made in regard to curricular activities of the school (e.g. home economics teachers being obliged to curtail their teaching hours in the subject)". (31)

WFP reported similar shortcomings in its health programme in Afghanistan — between 1972 and 1979, there was an average of 57,600 recipients a year in a programme costing WFP alone a total of $10.5 million.

> "The distribution of rations by the medical and paramedical staff of the institutions takes a considerable portion of their time, often at the expense of carrying out their other duties. . . As a result of the administrative burden faced by medical and paramedical staff most institutions failed to keep proper records of cases of malnourishment, and food stuffs were therefore often distributed without regard to malnourishment." (32)

Maxwell indicates that this problem is shared by all personnel associated with food distribution, ranging from "planners, administrators and nutritionists at the central government level . . . to school teachers and workers in health clinics, who are expected to service supplementary feeding programmes in addition to their normal duties". (33) He quotes a report which relates

> ". . . the misery of the teachers responsible for the school lunch programme in Orissa, with no government grant for a cook and no assistance with the administrative burdens of food collection or storage; the general impression is that there is little time for actual teaching. Similar effects may be found in health clinics, which leaves the net effect of supplementary feeding very much in question." (34)

In this way, development projects lose the benefit of the skills of many of the field workers they employ. Engaging extra staff for the purpose of distributing food aid might be an acceptable option but only when projects show a distinct likelihood of achieving their targets, since it would increase overheads substantially.

Recipient governments also make large financial contributions to projects.

For example, the Mauritanian Government is spending $690,000 a year to support a WFP school feeding programme. To transport, store and deliver $1.2 million of food aid over a period of two years and nine months cost a total of $2.4 million, $1.9 million of which was met by the Government. [35] Yet, the WFP report notes, "purchases of local foods [to be included in the school-lunch] are very limited because of shortage of funds". [36]

Government money spent on food aid projects is not necessarily unavailable for alternative development work. Choices have to be made on the basis of relative benefits. The following example from India illustrates this point.

> "People work out feeding programs at a cost of $x per recipient per year, with y recipients; they then tell us that for only $xy we can solve a large share of the country's nutritional problems. But $xy in India usually comes to a figure of hundreds of millions. An important question is whether India can afford simply to give away $200 million or $400 million in a feeding program; whether, if such sums are available, they should not be used as the wages of useful employment that creates durable assets." [37]

The AID evaluation on school feeding in India also argues that "it is very important that the benefits from the feeding program be weighed against alternative uses for these resources". [38] In some cases, a fraction of the money spent by donors on buying and transporting the food could be better invested in development projects which are likely to become independent of foreign assistance. [39] Some supplementary feeding programmes could be run more cheaply if they used locally available foods. Stevens illustrates for Botswana the economic feasibility of using such foods in place of WFP commodities:

> "In Botswana, the primary school lunch ration is 150 grammes CSM/CSB (corn soya blend) and 15 grammes of vegetable oil per child per day. It has been calculated that the corn soya milk could be replaced by a mixture of maize (65 per cent) and cow peas (35 per cent) which would have almost identical nutritional properties. The notional WFP value of this ration is some R11.38 per year; the local replacement cost of the proxy ration is only R5.58. Although maize is an acceptable nutritional substitute, it requires more processing that CSM, and the cost of this has to be taken into account." [40]

It has also been calculated that it costs twice as much to provide Indian school children with milk through food aid as it would through making local purchases.

> "The American farmer receives approximately 25 cents US for a litre of milk. It costs 8 cents for processing, another 7 cents for transportation including trucking and various shipping charges to India. Another 6 cents is added to the cost when you consider CARE's administration, the reimbursement for that from the government of West Bengal and the various American bureaucrats who also 'nurse' the milk along the way.

Finally, CARE pays 13 cents per litre . . . . to Mother Milk Dairy. This adds up to a total cost of 60 cents per litre. . . just under twice as much that Mother Milk Dairy charges for its own processed milk in the Calcutta market place." (41)

To make use of local foods whenever possible would keep costs down as well as positively promoting long-term development initiatives. It would also reduce the danger of a project's becoming dependent on supplies of exotic blended foods which, as Stevens says, "are not available outside the realm of food aid". (42)

Conclusions

The poor performance of supplementary feeding programmes in nutritional and educational terms means that they have proved highly expensive and inefficient. At present, a vast amount of money is spent each year on transporting and distributing food aid to people who are **not** malnourished. The efficiency of such programmes might be improved if they were effectively targeted and supervised, as was discussed in Chapter 4. This would entail an increase in administrative overheads, at least in the initial stages, but such projects would be judged by the quality of their performance as nutrition intervention measures rather than by the number of people they claimed to feed.

FFW projects are often deficient in the planning and securing of long-term benefits. In some cases, money is needed more urgently than food and would make a more appropriate contribution to development. Food commodities can be most effectively invested as relief items in disasters, when they directly answer a need.

The associated costs of project food aid, particularly transport and administration, have been subject to sharp increases in recent years. Transport costs would be reduced if donors made local or regional purchases of food whenever possible. Often, foods suitable for supplementary feeding can be produced from within the recipient country. In view of current inflationary trends, it would seem prudent to make long-term investments in such schemes to avoid dependence on supplies of foreign foods.

The distribution of food aid to individual recipients makes extensive and mundane demands on the time of skilled personnel. The opportunity cost of project food aid is, then, high.

As a tool for development, therefore, project food aid has proved to be expensive and inefficient.

7 THE *MANAGEMENT* OF FOOD AID

*M*anagement problems in food aid programmes are many and various. They range from breakdowns, such as the failure to supply spare parts for transport vehicles, to the issue of whether a project is ultimately of benefit to the poor. This chapter concentrates on three major problems:

- First, the practical difficulty of ensuring that large consignments of food from Europe and North America arrive on time in the villages for which they are destined. Given the complexities of handling and moving huge quantities of food across the world, food aid can be a logistical nightmare for everyone involved.
- Second, the need to ensure that targeting is accurate and that distribution is efficiently monitored.
- Third, the fundamental conceptual problem. Food distribution must be integrated with both short-term relief and long-term development objectives. It is only when these aims are clearly defined and understood that the validity of a food-aided project in development terms can be evaluated.

Logistical Problems

It is easy to sympathise with officials faced with organising the transport and distribution of bulky, perishable and easily misappropriated commodities which need careful supervision and comprehensive infrastructural support such as warehousing, vehicles and security. For example, a WFP-funded supplementary feeding programme in Pakistan, which began in July 1976 at a cost of $19 million over a four year period, had, as its broad objectives, a reduction in the high incidence of malnutrition amongst preschool children and expectant and nursing mothers, the promotion of better feeding practices through nutrition education and an increase in attendances at health centres with a consequent improvement in the health of the beneficiaries. Three schemes were to be launched to reach a total of 550,000 people. In 1980 WFP reported:

> "For several reasons the original commitment [of food aid], which was expected to be utilized in one year, could not be consumed in even three years, viz:
>
> a) Scheme A faced major difficulties in implementation and could therefore absorb only a fraction of the envisaged quantities of commodities. In the beginning there were shortages of counterpart funds for transport and personnel. WFP shipments arrived too early, thus allowing the project authorities too little time to prepare for imple-

mentation and to make adequate budgetary allocations. Also, since the project was planned for one year only, the project authorities hesitated to make financial allocations for the following year. Until recently, Kashmir could not provide funds for the transport of wheat and distributed only dried skim milk and butter oil. Food allocations to provinces and centres were not always made proportionately to the stipulated ration scale leading to an early exhaustion of under-allocated foodstuffs. Also, whenever only one commodity was available at the centres distribution was stopped. The slow start of the project necessitated loans and transfers of dried skim milk and butter oil to other WFP-assisted projects in Pakistan in order to avoid losses. However, when the project gained pace and Scheme A was ready to absorb more quantities, timely repayments could not be made and new shipments were not yet forthcoming . . .

b) Scheme B did not fully materialize. When WFP-supplied wheat reached the centres, CARE was already terminating the distribution of WSDM [whey-soy drink mix] and vegetable oil. In Baluchistan there was hardly any centre where wheat was distributed together with food from CARE for more than two months, and in Sind WFP wheat arrived when CARE food was no longer available. For these and other reasons, the quantities of wheat distributed were very limited.

c) Scheme C has never been implemented. Responsibility for its implementation changed during the planning stage. Finally, when a firm had been identified for the manufacture of 'PROTOLAC' [a low-cost, protein-rich food mixture] its capacity was found to be inadequate for the quantities envisaged." (1)

Although most other food projects will not experience as many problems as this one, the example illustrates what can go wrong with the ambitious goal of turning food aid into development; the problems for this project occurred **before** the development aspect had begun.

These logistical difficulties are not confined either to country, agency or project-type. For example, a WFP FFW scheme to construct mule trails and a jeep track in the hills of Nepal was planned to last five years and cost WFP $3.7 million with the local government contributing over $960,000 more.

The progress report submitted after two years and two months made the following comment:

"Another problem faced by the project insofar as WFP operations are concerned has been the late arrival of WFP commodities. Since commencement of the project only one shipment from a donor country has been received at the time requested. Shipments have not only arrived many months after required, but also different commodities have arrived at widely different times." (2)

US Government auditors were told by officials in Kerala, India, that,

Large consignments of food aid can place heavy demands on local transport and storage facilities. In the extreme case of Kampuchea in 1979-80, urgent emergency relief food could not be delivered until fleets of trucks were provided.

"... because the State Government is very poor, it will only authorize shipments of full truck-loads of grain or oil from the depot to district or subdistrict level. Moreover, once the grain or oil reaches the district or subdistrict level, it is not redistributed, for the same reasons of economy. We were told that this situation tends to result in the grains being shipped to one end of the State and oil to another. As a result, both CARE and CRS were experiencing a widespread lack of oil ...

We noted that some district and subdistrict storage areas had no oil in stock. Other areas had large stocks of oil which had not been distributed because of inadequate grain supplies to distribute. Still other locations had almost no grain or oil. [One] CARE warehouse contained 76 cartons of oil ... but only 75 bags of title II blended foods ... Similarly, a CRS warehouse ... had 3000 bags of grain, but had been out of oil for three months. Yet, other CARE and CRS warehouses that we visited in Kerala had large stocks of grain or oil, or both." (3)

That there is **too much** food aid is also one of the managerial problems to be faced. The US must, by congressional mandate, deliver a minimum mandated tonnage of project food aid each year, whether it is needed or not. By 1982, 1.7 million tons must be distributed. In 1979, the US Government auditors described the difficulties the mandate had caused:

"The minimum tonnage distribution requirement is also putting pressure on AID and the volags to distribute more commodities. For example, India officials recently told the volags that they would assume responsibility for much of the volag food-for-work programs. This decision was apparently designed to use up some of India's existing wheat surpluses, which are becoming huge. As soon as this decision had been made, however, AID and the volags programed substantial increases for MCH and school feeding in India which essentially made up for the shortage. This indicated that the desire to maintain existing worldwide program levels because of the minimum tonnage requirement was a strong motivating force in reprograming. AID officials acknowledged that without the India reprogramings, they could not have met the legislated minimum." (4)

The EEC does not manage its own projects but hands over the food aid to governments and other agencies such as the WFP. In their *Special Report on Community Food Aid,* the EEC auditors noted that:

"750 tonnes of milk powder sent as emergency aid were still not used two months after arrival as the recipient country did not have the necessary means of transport.

The same delivery suffered seriously in unloading because the port had no handling equipment.

In one country 100 out of 500 tonnes of milk powder were dumped into the sea for lack of means of transport. . .

250 out of 500 tonnes of vitaminized milk delivered to an organization were still in store in insecure conditions five months later. The Commission delegate wrote that a large proportion of the sacks were torn and milk was being thrown away by the tonne. . . .

In many cases use of the aid is put at risk because neither the local authorities nor the Commission delegate are informed beforehand when ships are to arrive." (5)

Quite apart from failing to attain its immediate objectives, food aid which goes astray in this way is expensive in time, manpower and administrative costs and makes no direct contribution to development.

Targeting and Monitoring

Concern about the lack of accurate and adequate reporting and monitoring pervades a great many project food aid documents. Stevens reports that in both Upper Volta and Tunisia, systematic records of deliveries of food aid to individual institutions are not kept. (6) In Upper Volta, "it is difficult to obtain any useful data on the distribution of food for nutrition" and no records are available on participants in FFW schemes. (7) Work records are not collated for FFW in Lesotho. (8) On MCH programmes, ". . . in none of the four countries studied are records kept to indicate supply and demand . . ." (9)

A lack of reporting means that serious divergences may exist between the theory and the practice of a given project. This is illustrated by an account of a WFP project in Brazil intended to provide nutrition education and supplementary feeding to primary school children.

"Record keeping, accounting, data retrieval and analysis, and information generally available to enable management to control proper distribution of food and planning for the replenishment of stock centrally and in schools are all seriously inadequate. There even seemed to be a lack of full understanding at certain levels that the rate of utilization of WFP commodities is much lower than planned." (10)

Lack of adequate planning on FFW projects may mean that work-norms have not been established or that rations are not standardised. A progress report on a WFP project in Sri Lanka illustrates the former.

"In the formative stage of the schemes, estimates were made of the man-days required to carry them out in conformity with standard work norms. As rations are distributed for days worked, food is allocated on the basis of these estimates. Not infrequently, they have been far off the mark, resulting in over or under-allocations of food. Where the estimates were too high, it appears that in many cases the entire excessive allocation was nevertheless distributed. The mission has the impression that the estimates were often made 'from the desk', without field survey." (11)

An interim evaluation of a WFP project in Senegal exemplifies the operational difficulties of standardising rations.

". . . the mission found that the ration scale was quite often not adhered to, the reasons being either a wrong interpretation of the instructions, or the feeling that the established ration was insufficient, or because the exact calculation for the number of man-days worked appeared to be too time-consuming. The ration actually distributed varied between one fourth and 10 times the stipulated family ration. While these are extreme cases, there was a general tendency to distribute an increased ration." (12)

An evaluation team in Honduras was unable to find sufficient data on file and, in order to begin work, had to develop original information in or from the feeding centres. Its report to AID noted that:

"While there are occasional supervisory visits on the part of CARE, a review of the supervisory reports which had been made on the centers visited by the team indicate that every report stated that conditions were satisfactory. However, the team found that the conditions in many centers were far below the standards which were required and should have been reported as such in the supervisory report." (13)

Similarly, field workers in the Caribbean checked the application lists for MCH food aid and found that "not **one** single list was correct, names of non-existent people, 'pregnant mothers' sixty years old, etc., etc.".(14)

Describing a field trip to MCH centres in the Dominican Republic, an AID official noted in his report:

"Many regular recipients were interviewed, and the survey discloses that: (1)They do not know where the food comes from. (2)They do not know why they are receiving it. (3)They have not received visit[s] from the social workers' group. (4) They do not receive enough food." (15)

In Bangladesh, the author of an AID report described what happened when he went to evaluate a water tank project in Pabna. "A visit to that embankment revealed that although it was reported completed it was not." (16) Another tank was, therefore, chosen for the evaluation. "The project was reported completed, but in fact very little earthwork was done." (17)

One reason for the inadequacy of much of the reporting is that, at times, field workers are simply unable to account for the food.

"Even CARE's field representative for emergency relief in Uganda admitted, 'there are no controls. We don't know what happens to the food after it is distributed to the local leaders'." (18)

Occasionally, large amounts of food are lost through rotting, bad storage, etc. More often, the losses arise through 'misappropriation'. In some countries, this reaches alarming proportions. In Bangladesh, estimates of the percentage of misappropriated food aid vary from 30% to 75%. The 1979 AID report on FFW in Bangladesh found that, unless there was some basic error in the data, there was "a very strong indication that less than 70% of the wheat withdrawn for FFW finds its way to the laborers". (19) Thus of the 240,000 tons of wheat used in the 1979 dry-season for FFW, at least 72,000 might have gone astray.

Labourers on a FFW project in Bangladesh were asked if they had benefited from the work. "No, they said, **their** lives hadn't improved [now there was a new road] ; all they knew was that they were supposed to be paid six pounds of wheat a day and they'd only got three. No one saw any accounts. No one knew what had happened to the rest of the food." (20) The AID/Bangladesh report mentioned above urged the case more strongly.

> "It's been concluded that the project records at present cannot be expected to reflect the actual facts regarding a project and therefore cannot be used as a basis for supervision. On the contrary the inherently false recording works more as a loophole for misappropriation." (21)

The former principal WFP officer for 23 African countries echoed this conclusion.

> "A great number of annual audited accounts (possibly most – if not all) about utilisation of our main resources – food – are presented from the field with the inclusion of manipulated figures." (22)

Losses, he stated, including diversions and unauthorised distribution and sales, were often many times greater than were reported and accounts were "fiction". (23) Moreover, the easy misappropriation actually encouraged dishonesty. Another food aid official described how this could happen:

> "In almost every country that I have been in, the tendency is for the Project Manager, once he is appointed, to bring in all his closest relatives. The whole set-up becomes a family affair. Even if store keepers and field inspectors were not basically corrupt, they would soon be, for the manager quickly finds many lucrative ways of utilising WFP commodities and his storekeepers are obliged to obey all his orders (for the illegal disposal of WFP commodities) or go." (24)

In Ghana, the large-scale misappropriation of food aid sent after a drought in 1977, eventually led to its discontinuation there. (25)

In Haiti, misappropriation takes place at all levels. In late 1978, an OXFAM staff member commented:

> "I was watching an American brother overseeing the distribution of food aid to a group of workers on an FFW project. Oil and three types of food were being handed out by the foreman, who organised the work party. The brother had a clip board

and conscientiously ticked off each allocation against each worker's name.

He said he tried to do the job carefully because the food had been given by American taxpayers. I asked how he set about estimating whether the work done was a full day's work and he said that he trusted the foreman to do that. I noticed that as a particular group of workers came round for each food item someone would distract the brother's attention while the foreman whipped extra portions into their bags. I asked the brother if every worker was supposed to get the same ration and he said 'yes'. 'In that case you're being cheated by your foreman', I replied. He admitted that this was possible and added that he always took the precaution of paying out less than the proper daily rate to the workers to make up for it. In other words, both sides, the brother and the workers, were on the fiddle!" (26)

Elsewhere in Haiti, food aid has often disappeared before it reached its destination. In 1978, food aid workers in Port-au-Prince spoke of a certain street corner where lorries slow down allowing people waiting for them to remove entire sacks of food aid. (27) This was apparently quite common practice. In Haiti, only food from Germany is apparently delivered in reasonable quantities to the correct recipients. Losses are between 20% and 30%, and are considered to be much lower than those suffered by other agencies. (28)

It is impossible to eradicate misappropriation. As Stevens comments, "nothing falls off the back of a lorry more easily than a sack of food aid!" (29) Lack of reporting makes misappropriation even easier. However, the fact that the food is free encourages what the donors call corruption. Free gifts cannot be stolen. When the food arrives in large amounts without careful attention to need or the level of local production, it is not surprising that it is treated casually. When the need is greater, the temptation to divert supplies for profit is natural, and only the most stringent monitoring will ensure that all the food reaches those for whom it is intended. Losses are frequently high. The EEC auditors noted that,

". . . during a visit by the Court, the local authorities agreed that out of 1,000 tonnes of cereals provided free by the Community 44% disappeared en route or rotted in store. . ." (30)

The problem might be alleviated if the food were sold rather than given away as this would encourage proper accounting. However, the size of the programmes — involving millions of people — tends to diminish the chances of effective monitoring and supervision.

The Conceptual Problem: Programme Objectives and Evaluation

Project food aid is an attempt to turn a relief item into a tool for long-term development. It is commodity-oriented, an indirect approach to the problems of poverty and malnutrition. The food could be seen as an advantage, since it can be used as a flexible component in projects as varied as providing food supplements to school children or as payment to workers on land-improvement schemes. However, this flexibility may act as a double disadvantage; firstly, it encourages people to think that the food can do more than merely feed people, and secondly, it encourages the thought that food-aided projects can simultaneously fulfil several quite different objectives. Vagueness with regard to goals compounds the practical difficulty of ensuring effective monitoring, and in turn the possibility of qualitative and decisive evaluations is further delayed. As a result, projects may drift on without ever proving their claims and without being challenged. For example, the US Mid Day Meal programme in India has been in existence for 20 years and at its peak, in 1978, was reaching over 11 million children. However, as an AID report noted in 1980:

> "One of the most frequently cited reasons for supporting the Mid Day Meal Program is its impact on the enrolment of disadvantaged children in school. It is astonishing that this relationship has **never** been analyzed." [31]

It is a responsibility of the donors to guarantee that food aid is used properly. To do this, projects need regular evaluation not only of their objectives but also of their social and economic impact. However,

> "WFP does not have the capacity to monitor closely the economic and social aspects of the projects it assists. Furthermore, government ministries and agencies responsible for project implementation and monitoring in the poorest countries to which most WFP aid is directed may not have the financial and human resources for frequent assessment of a project's progress, especially social assessment, beyond the minimum required for their six-monthly or yearly reports to WFP headquarters." [32]

And the EEC auditors stress the urgent need to check "that aid does effectively meet the needs that it is intended to meet". [33] However, they add that,

> ". . . in view of the inadequacy of local administrations and of the reports provided by recipients, attainment of this latter objective will remain illusory unless there is to be an army of Community auditors." [34]

On available evidence, the performance of the Indian school feeding programme would not justify the cost of a thorough evaluation, were it possible to make one. The AID report cited above says:

> "First, the data to adequately identify the impacts are simply, for the most part, unavailable. The feeding program started in India nearly two decades ago. How it has affected attendance rates, health status, and academic performance will remain shrouded in darkness in the absence of baseline and longitudinal data.
>
> Second, the feeding program is expensive relative to India's per student investment in primary education. The program would have to have had a fairly substantial impact on objectives

such as enrolment and attendance to be cost-effective. The evaluation work to date does not make one sanguine about finding such evidence." (35)

When records do exist, they may not provide the information that is required to chart the success of a project. As a WFP general review states:

"A simple count of the number of food recipients in a supplementary feeding project may show that targets have been met, when the actual **objective** of the project — to improve the nutritional status of the poorest sector — has not." (36)

Definition of objectives can often prove to be over-ambitious or confused. The UNICEF survey on supplementary feeding programmes noted:

"We would argue that a serious failing of many programs now operating is that the real objectives have not been clearly identified and probably have not been sufficiently considered in program design." (37)

In some cases, the short-term and long-term goals of programmes are of doubtful practical and conceptual compatibility — for example, the integration of education about improved dietary habits and gifts of food. A WFP paper expresses this problem.

"Given that most supplementary feeding projects designed for nutritional crisis intervention have difficulty, for a number of valid reasons, even delivering the basic health and nutrition services they are assumed to provide, the expectation that they can also be linked to major educational, training, or income-generating activities is probably unrealistic. It may be better to keep the two types of activities conceptually (and programmatically) distinct." (38)

These contradictions highlight the differences between relief feeding and development work and suggest that the donors have difficulty in reconciling the two aspects. Evaluations, particularly those made on behalf of the US Government, often comment on the lack of clear objectives and a failure to put these in order of priority. In the case of US food aid, this is attributed in part to the conflicting purposes of the whole programme, as defined by Title II of PL 480. (39) Inevitably, such conflict underlies the selection and management of individual projects.

In 1979, US Government auditors made the following observations on the basis of field work in six countries:

"Our review shows that the title II program is not adequately reaching poorer countries or the needier people in the six countries we visited, particularly rural areas and the high priority MCH category. Nor is this food assistance being planned or programed in a way to contribute to the overall development process in these countries. Instead, the program is today being driven more by infrastructure availability or limitations, and, to an extent, commodity availability, than by real needs." (40)

Conclusions

There are a great many links in the food aid chain, the failure of any one of which can seriously upset the performance of a given project. Whereas international food traders may have similar logistical problems to those facing the managers of food aid, their job is much simpler because they have only to transport the food to the country in question. Project food aid tries to go two steps further; firstly, it is destined for individual recipients, and secondly, it is intended to act as a stimulus to or instrument of development.

In addition, commercial distributors are governed at each stage by the legalities relating to their transactions. Commodities may go astray but someone will be answerable for them. Food aid, by contrast, is a free gift which makes it far less accountable.

There have been calls by some major donors for improvements in handling food aid. The EEC auditors conclude their section on the purchasing, loading, transport and distribution of food aid with the recommendation that "programming and management of Community food aid need to be completely recast". (41) The US Government auditors made a similar recommendation in saying that "fundamental changes are needing in the way title II [project food aid] is programed and administered at the country level". (42) However, the question remains whether it is always economically practicable to follow the complex and exhaustive administrative procedures necessary to ensure the food reaches the people for whom it is intended, and has the results intended. Where the food is really needed — as in the case of refugee relief — the effort must be made, but where the end results are in question, the expense would seem scarcely justifiable.

Inadequate reporting means that food aid continues to be given without knowledge of what it does or even what it is meant to do. Misappropriation and illegal sales are widespread; evaluations have often failed to confirm the assumptions on which the projects actually rest and have even shown them to be doing more harm than good. At other times what effects the food may have had are simply not known. An evaluator who spent nearly five months reviewing CRS food aid projects in Central America and the Caribbean made the following comment:

> "The food goes out and doubtless, the majority of it is consumed. But the overall impression one obtains from visits in the region and from talking to CRS field staff, is that the whole thing is such a gigantic operation that no-one can really know what is happening at the end of the line." (43)

In similar fashion, the 1979 AID-funded evaluation of project food aid in India — then involving over 19,000,000 recipients — noted that it "started with the means, food, some 25 years ago and has been seeking an end ever since". (44)

Such shortcomings will be hard to avoid. Often programmes are so vast that to monitor and adequately to evaluate them would require a disproportionate expenditure of money. It is unlikely that either donor or recipient governments would find the resources to undertake such supervision.

Finally, project food aid has been in existence for over 25 years. So far, no way has been found to solve the inherent serious and perennial management problems outlined in this chapter. At the very least, they call into question the usefulness of project food aid as a tool for development.

8 PROJECT FOOD AID AS COMPETITION WITH LOCAL FOOD PRODUCTION

One of the American PL 480 programme's professed principal aims is the expansion of markets for US agricultural products. Another is encouraging development in countries determined to improve their own agricultural production. It is doubtful whether these two aims can ever be compatible. More attention has been focussed on the potential disincentive effects of food aid on local agriculture than on any other aspect of food aid. [1] The availability of large quantities of free or concessionally priced imported food may depress the price of local food. This, it is argued, will lead to reduced production. To date, this concern has related to the bulk donation and concessional sales programmes carried out on a government-to-government basis. It has generally been assumed that the smaller, more targeted project food aid could have little effect on the local market and therefore on production.

The present methods of assessing the potential effects of food aid on local production are imprecise; a comparison is made between the total tonnage of food aid and the gross food production of a country. [2] This does not give an accurate reflection of the extent to which **local** markets are affected. It has been argued that a better comparison is between the volume of food aid and the proportion of local produce that enters the domestic market.

> "The displacement of local produce and the disincentive effect occurs solely in the markets, and for a majority of these countries it is true to say that there is a relatively close relationship between the percentage of non-agricultural population on the one hand and the proportion of market production as a percentage of overall output on the other. Percentages are more or less evenly matched, so if 10 to 15 per cent of a country's population are not engaged in agriculture then only about 10 to 15 per cent of overall food output will be channelled via the market. 3 per cent [of food aid imports] in relation to this much smaller marketed percentage naturally presents an altogether different picture. In the 10 to 15 per cent instance food aid would correspond to between 20 and 30 per cent of local market production. This comparison alone is relevant in assessing possible negative influences." [3]

In making this calculation, it is also essential to consider the total food aid entering an area, not merely the amount donated by an individual agency.

There are two major distinctions between government-to-government and project food aid. Firstly, the latter is provided in small quantities relative to national production and other imports. Secondly, project food aid is not meant to enter the market; its distribution through development projects is intended to ensure that food is either reaching people who could not otherwise earn the money to buy it (FFW) or that it is supplementing the normal diets of people who need more to eat than they can afford (MCH and school feeding). The late Executive Director of the WFP argued that, "WFP. . . avoids the risk of reducing farm incomes by concentrating exclusively on food aid projects in which the commodities are distributed at the very point where they are earned and consumed, usually far from urban centres, and in circumstances where the additional food results only in additional local consumption, without depressing the markets that guide agricultural producers". (4)

Nevertheless there is some evidence to suggest that project food aid competes with local production in three ways:

1) It causes lower consumption of local food, thereby taking buyers out of the local market.

2) It draws people away from agricultural work.

3) It requires the same resources as local agriculture (storage, transport etc.). It is the direct **competition** with local production, rather than the vaguer concept of "disincentive" that should be examined in relation to project food aid.

Taking Buyers Out of the Market

In supplementary feeding, the substitution of food aid for local food is common (see Chapters 4 and 5). The 1977 five-country CARE report estimated that substitution rates in three of the countries ranged from 39%–69%. (5) People therefore spent less money on buying local food. The same report found that:

> "In all five countries mothers stated that they were able to spend less on foods for their families since being enrolled in the CARE feeding program. . . The high rates of substitution of the ration for the home diet which were found also serve as proof of the savings resulting from participation in the program." (6)

A nutritional survey in Northern Ghana examined the relationship between consumption of local foods and 'supplementary' feeding.

> ". . . there was a reduction in the consumption of various foods in Toma the week following the clinic in comparison to the week before the clinic. Among the pre-school children there was a reduction in the consumption of dried fish, cow's milk, groundnuts, acha porridge, boiled yams, roasted yam and fufu after the clinic food was received. Among the lactating women there was a reduction in the amount of dried fish, acha porridge, okra, tomatoes, onions, yam slices, roasted yam and fufu consumed. Among the pregnant women there was a reduction in the amount of dried fish, groundnuts, acha tuon saffi, dawadawa, neri and hibiscus leaves consumed." (7)

At least some of those foods would have been bought in the market.

An evaluation carried out in 1977 by CRS in Guatemala examined the savings that workers on a FFW scheme had been able to make.

> "Everyone who replied [to the questionnaire] stated that they had saved on food purchases by using Title II foodstuffs. . . Substantial savings were made in regard to purchases of corn, beans and lard." (8)

Another way in which project food aid competes with local production is by entering the market. Sales are reported to be particularly prevalent in two of the 'hungriest' nations in the world — Haiti and Bangladesh. In Haiti in 1978 officials estimated that between 50 percent and 80 percent of project food aid was sold. (9) A team of American and Haitian development workers surveyed 3 markets in the North-west of the country and estimated that one market contained 25 percent US project food aid, another 40 percent and the third a "large percentage". (10) /A UN official described these sales as "rampant". (11)

In 1979, WFP estimated that of its annual commitment of 100,000 tonnes to Bangladesh "roughly 30,000 metric tons are being sold by workers, plus an unknown amount of misappropriated wheat". (12) While most aid workers would agree that individual recipients should be free to use a proportion of their rations to obtain other necessities, the effect of substantial sales on the local economy is a serious concern. When it occurs on a large scale it calls into question the real need for aid in the form of food.

Drawing People Away from Agricultural Work

As a consequence of this market competition, producers may be discouraged from growing more than their immediate needs. Workers on a FFW project in Haiti claimed that they relied on the money raised by selling their food aid and so did not plant as much in their gardens the following year. (13) In addition, there was a shortage of agricultural labour because so many people were occupied with the FFW scheme. (14) Farmers in the Highlands of Guatemala made similar complaints about the relief efforts following the earthquake of 1976. (15)

Over a longer period of time, the availability of food aid can discourage husbandry of existing crops and the planting of new ones. For example, the former head of WFP's West Africa programme stated that in 1976 a government field officer from one African country reported to his Department of Agriculture:

> "The sorghums and especially millets have yielded poorly because of the priority given by farmers to groundnuts. Cereals were generally weeded very late and in many cases not at all.
> This problem of priority for groundnuts is the result of past food aid programmes. They create and foster a dependency in farmers' minds on food aid being provided year after year."
> (16)

A missionary in Ghana reports the unintended effects on local farmers of a consignment of food aid which a colleague had arranged to be delivered.

> "The following year he discovered that the people he had

Large consignments of food aid can compete with food grown locally. When local food prices fall farmers (and the landless labourers they usually employ) are both affected.

'helped', expecting the same help the following year, had sown less grain in time for the rains. This was to be his first and last attempt." (17)

Stevens provides data showing that between 1960 and 1970, the amount of fallow land in Lesotho increased by 26 per cent; the proportion of small-holdings (less than 2 acres) lying fallow also increased. (18) A worker with a 1.2 acre holding would need to participate in a FFW project for only 5 months a year to equal his possible farm income. (19) If more than one member of his family is a food aid recipient — and according to 1979 figures, at least half the population are recipients of US food aid — then it would take even less time to acquire the same amount of food as they could produce themselves. (20) Although it cannot be concluded that food aid has encouraged the trend towards increasing fallow land in Lesotho, a 1980 evaluation from WFP lends weight to the contention.

> "However, in spite of efforts not to employ an excessive number of people in any given village at peak periods, a strong risk of market displacement still exists, since people seem to prefer to receive food aid rather than produce their own food in their own fields with the considerable risks inherent in Lesotho agriculture." (21)

It is worth noting that food aid to Lesotho has increased considerably in recent years. Between 1975 and 1979, the number of **FFW** recipients of US food aid went up by 30 per cent and now represents about 20 per cent of the population. (22)

Competition for Resources

Food aid requires the same infrastructure as local produce, particularly for storage and transport. This brings it into competition for scarce resources. For example, in Haiti a substantial proportion of the local crop is reported to be lost each year through inadequate storage. (23) This is one of the reasons why peasant farmers are forced to sell their produce immediately after the harvest, when prices are at their lowest. An annual report from one of the major food aid agencies there states:

> "The availability of grain storage for farmers in rural Haiti is of vital importance because of the large annual fluctuations in grain prices caused by speculation and drought and because of the incredible damage done by rodents to grain that is improperly stored." (24)

The urgent need for improved decentralised storage was the subject of a meeting of peasant farmers attended by the author in 1978. Despite this, in the same year, 14 large centralised warehouses for food aid imported by CARE and WFP were being built or planned at a cost of $1,271,000. (25) Once equipped with better storage, donors require improved transport facilities, as the 1978 CARE — Haiti Annual Report explained:

> "As CARE's food programs expand, there is also a greater need

for additional carrying capacity and additional personnel to oversee field performance. The additional field personnel, in turn, require additional vehicles to ensure adequate field coverage. As the number of the vehicles increase, so does the need for professional fleet management and maintenance." (26)

To meet those expanding needs, four additional trucks were bought and thirteen new staff taken on at a cost of $159,000. (27) WFP's programme called for $556,000 to be spent over several years on transporting its food within Haiti. (28) In addition, the Haitian Government was required to provide two 12-ton lorries. (29) Thus, in this case, it seems clear that food aid is in direct competition with local produce for storage and transport all the way from the field to the market. As such problems affect farmers in many parts of the world – particularly in Africa – the accumulated results of such competition should not be ignored. Moreover, peasant farmers are most affected by this, since large companies usually produce export crops. Peasant farmers also take on seasonal labour so that if production was reduced in response to an influx of food aid, it is this poorer section of the population which would be most affected.

Conclusions

Since project food aid aims to reach individual recipients, it is at the local level that disruptions in the domestic economy will be felt first. For local farmers, therefore, the principal side effects of such projects are likely to be market competition with sales of food aid and a reduction in consumer demand as a result of the substitution of imports for local foods. Farmers may also be at a disadvantage because of the resources required by imported food aid: it may be simpler for governments to accept food aid than to assist local producers.

While it is difficult to prove conclusively that food aid is necessarily a disincentive to local production, it is clear that there are several ways in which it does affect it. Indeed, as it becomes institutionalised, so it requires an infrastructure of its own and thus competes with local farmers for facilities essential to both.

Finally, with the possible exception of resettlement programmes, it is hard to see where food aid has provided a positive **incentive** to local small farmer production.

In conclusion, then, there is evidence to dispute the generally accepted belief that the risk of disincentive to domestic food production is avoided when food aid is targeted at particular groups or specific projects. This belief is in fact no more than an assumption.

9 CONCLUSIONS

The problems associated with project food aid outlined in this book are not new. They have been identified by many different groups over a large number of years. Not only have field workers and on-the-spot evaluators found much to question, but staff of aid agencies and the governments that give them the food have made many of the most telling criticisms.

Despite these frequent expressions of concern, food aid administrators still defend the principle of project food aid. In the main they have not yet accepted our finding that food is, by its nature, an inappropriate form of development assistance. Attention is paid to questions of how to improve its delivery, while we argue that, except for a limited range of relief needs, large-scale food aid should be substantially reduced.

As evidence is presented against the efficacy of food aid in one form of development assistance after another, new rationales for its continued use are produced. Some commentators have claimed benefits other than the now questionable ones of nutrition or development. Stevens, for example, concludes his study by arguing the "the real impact of food aid can be quite different from its apparent effects", and by stating that project food aid "is best thought of as income-in-kind". [1] This argument minimises the importance of competition with local production inherent in providing food aid in non-disaster times. Food aid's tendency to create dependence on imported commodities, to devalue local products in the eyes of the recipients and thus to work against development also diminishes the strength of this argument. The fact that projects are often not targeted satisfactorily in **economic** terms – as with millions of schoolchildren, for example – further weakens the case. Finally, the cost in staff and cash terms needs to be considered. Time, manpower and money would be much better spent on helping the really needy and in devising sound development efforts. The income-in-kind argument is an apology for food aid, rather than a point in its favour.

It has been argued that the case against food aid is no different from the case against development assistance generally. It is not our concern here to argue for or against aid as such. It is our view, however, that there are inherent problems associated with food aid which are peculiar to it and make it a particularly cumbersome and inappropriate means of providing assistance. On the surface project food aid seem to provide a morally and politically acceptable way of sharing the fruits of over-production in the North with those in need in the South. Because of its appeal at this simple level, and because of governments' interests in supporting their own rural economies, food aid's inherent weaknesses have been largely overlooked. But donors must recognise its ineffectiveness and the damage it can cause.

Why has this not been acknowledged already? Food aid is the prime example of an available commodity determining aid policy. As we noted earlier, the food aid tail wags the development dog. It is a commodity-oriented programme which starts with the food and then has to devise projects through which to distribute it. Given the difficulties of administering large-scale commodity aid, it is not surprising, on a practical level, that so few food-aided projects can demonstrate long-term success. Distribution not development becomes the overriding factor. The donor countries have food to dispose of. They seek acceptable ways of doing so. Development assistance seems an eminently acceptable solution. Frequently the details of the projects' development aims are seen as of secondary importance. The dilemma is well summed up in the AID-funded evaluation of the huge food aid programme in India:

> "The CARE program in India is almost exclusively concerned with food distribution and its other projects are primarily in support of its food program. Its cash expenditures are well integrated into food programs, as they go primarily for construction of balwadis [creches] and payment for support services for maternal-child feeding, food processing facilities, and godowns [warehouses] for storage of Title II food. A heavy focus of the CARE program is on moving the food, which entails considerable logistical effort, and which they do quite well. Unfortunately, this may distract attention from the broader development questions and limit activities in non-food programs." (2)

While a major donor such as the US has its food aid policies dictated by the requirements of a minimum mandated tonnage, it will be difficult to resolve this dilemma.

The major food aid agencies are vocal in their advocacy of the role of this form of aid. Given their substantial involvement in the business of distributing foods their arguments may not always be entirely disinterested.

Proponents of food aid often justify it as a short-term expedient. This has been its justification for over 25 years, long enough to turn rhetoric into reality, yet the tendency has been to institutionalise food aid-dependent projects. It is now time to begin closing them down. Since the really malnourished are not being reached by existing programmes in any significant way, closure will have no negative effects on them. Indeed it may have a positive benefit by enabling people to concentrate on more effective means of development.

Priorities for the use of food aid should then be revised. It should be used where it is genuinely irreplaceable, for refugees, for emergencies where food itself is in short supply and for the institutional feeding of the old, the sick and other welfare cases. In such circumstances, every effort must be made to ensure that food arrives on time and reaches the people who need it. To this end, procurement, delivery and distribution procedures need to be radically improved.

When, and only when, such needs have been satisfied should food aid be used for development, and then according to strict criteria. As with all forms of development assistance, project design should start with felt development needs that those it is intended to help can identify with. If food aid can then be used to facilitate such projects, it will be making a useful contribution. Food aid may be used to genuine nutritional advantage in a child health project which has identified a specific food need for the demonstrably malnourished that cannot be met locally. A resettlement project where preparation of a new site can only be done if outside food is available, a small-scale irrigation project where marginal farmers need support while they work together to build ditches – these are possible candidates for the effective use of food aid. Each project must have tangible and achievable objectives and not just broad conceptual 'development' ends. This will mean reducing drastically the number of people reached, but it is likely to mean that those reached are the people most genuinely in need, and that the help given will have a lasting effect. It can only be done if the prime aim is development assistance and not counting heads and bags of food.

Finite limits should be placed on the amount of food to be distributed and on the timing of the project to avoid institutionalisation of the food aid component. The discontinuation of food aid should be written into the project design. Finally, independent evaluations, with the power to affect future policy, are the only way of ensuring that food aid programmes are achieving the targets that have been set.

The inevitable outcome of this prescription would be that much less food aid would be needed. Welfare projects will only ever make relatively small demands, and more tightly controlled development projects will need less food inputs than the large-scale projects so prevalent at present. Pressures to increase the scale of food distribution beyond this should be resisted, regardless of the domestic political pressures on donor countries.

It has been assumed up to now that food aid is needed because there is a shortage of food in the Third World. The Third World is thus seen as a vast refugee camp with hungry people lining up for food from the global food aid soup kitchen. This view is false. Some disasters aside (and these are important areas for food aid), the basic problem is not one of food, but poverty. Free handouts of food do not address this problem, they aggravate it.

It may be going against the grain to call for a substantial reduction in non-emergency project food aid. However, analysis of the experience of the last 25 years suggests that it is time we did.

REFERENCES

REFERENCES CHAPTER 1

1. In 1980 $2,619,000,000 worth of food aid (net) was disbursed, according to the Organisation for Economic Co-operation and Development (OECD), in *1981 Review: Development Co-operation*, OECD, Paris, 1981, table A.10. See Appendix for details.

2. WFP/CFA (Committee on Food Aid Policies and Programmes): 9/5, "General Review of Food Aid Policies and Programmes", March 1980, p. 11.

3. Food for Peace, *1979 Annual Report on Public Law 480*, US Government Printing Office, Washington DC, 1981, Table 17. The actual figure given for all recipients of Title II (project) food aid is 66,360,899. Of these however just over 5,500,000 were included under a special sales pro-gramme of food aid and as such are not the subject of this report.

4. International Development and Food Assistance Act of 1977, US Congress, 1977.

5. "Statement by Mr Edouard Saouma, Director-General of the Food and Agriculture Organization of the United Nations, before the Committee on Development and Cooperation of the European Parliament, Brussels, 1 April 1980", p. 6.

6. *North-South: A programme for survival,* Independent Commission on International Development Issues, Pan Books, London, 1980, p. 104.

7. Comptroller General of the United States, *Changes Needed in the Administration of the Overseas Food Donation Program*, Report to the Congress, US General Accounting Office, Washington DC, 15 October 1979, p. 33.

8. Group for International Nutrition, Institute for Nutrition Research, University of Oslo, *Nordic Food Aid*, Nordic Council of Ministers Secretariat, Stockholm, 1980, p. 27.

9. Mrs K. Focke, "Working Document on an effective food aid policy that takes into account the needs of hunger-stricken countries and peoples — emergency aid", European Parliament Working Documents 1980–1981, Annex, 5 Sept. 1981, p. 56.

10. European Communities, Court of Auditors, *Special Report on Community Food Aid*, 30 October 1980, p. 118.

11. "EEC 21st Report: Development Aid Policy", *Hansard*, Vol. 420, No. 89, Col. 1302, 3 June 1981.

12. Jonathan Fryer, *Food for Thought, The Use and Abuse of Food Aid in the Fight Against World Hunger*, World Council of Churches, Geneva, 1981.

13. "Recommendations by the Canadian Council for International Co-operation on Food Issues to the Parliamentary Task Force on North South Relations", Ottawa, 1 October 1980, p. 2.

REFERENCES CHAPTER 2

1. WFP/CFA: 9/5, "General Review of Food Aid Policies & Programmes", March 1980, p. 11.

2. For a full account of the Ethiopian case, see Jack Shepherd, *The Politics of Starvation,* Carnegie Endowment for International Peace, Washington DC, 1975, p. 16. The writer concludes that,
"Ethiopia, in 1973, became an example of problems facing the international agencies on a global basis. These agencies and the donor nation administrators shared their unwillingness to sacrifice political considerations, in retrospect very short range, for humanitarian concerns of more enduring importance. In fact, the famine in Ethiopia shows us that those men and women whose job it is to handle drought and food emergencies or publicize outbreaks of disease are unwilling or unable to do so. . . . In Ethiopia, thousands of helpless peasants were sacrificed for this attitude." (pp. 81-82).

3. Richard W. Franke and Barbara H. Chasin, *Seeds of Famine,* Allanheld, Osmun and Co., Montclair, 1980, p. 11.

4. Hal Sheets and Roger Morris, *Disaster in the Desert: Failures of International Relief in the West African Drought,* Special Report, Humanitarian Policy Studies, Carnegie Endowment for International Peace, Washington DC, 1974, p. 2.

5. Christopher Stevens, *Food Aid and the Developing World,* Croom Helm/ Overseas Development Institute, London, 1979, p. 21. Stevens adds that further details of the part of the British Government in this affair can be found in the *Fifth Report from the Committee of Public Accounts, Session 1976-77,* HMSO, London, 23 June 1977, paras. 839-925.

6. Robin J. Biellik and Peggy L. Henderson, "Mortality, Nutritional Status and Dietary Conditions in a Food Deficit Region: North Teso District, Uganda, December, 1980", *Ecology of Food and Nutrition,* December 1981, p. 168.

7. Personal letter of 27 September 1978.

8. Jo Froman et al., "General Review: PL 480 Food Assistance in Guatemala", Antigua, Guatemala (mimeo) June 1977 (a). The authors worked as contractors for AID during 1976 and 1977 and the review is based on the AID/Guatemala files. The information regarding the release of supplies elsewhere in Latin America is taken from House of Representatives, *Managing International Disasters: Guatemala. Hearings and Markup before the . . . Committee on International Relations,* HR 12046, US Government Printing Office, Washington DC, 1976, p. 33.

9. Robert Gersony et al., *A Contrastive Analysis of Alternative Reconstruction Models after the February 1976 Guatemalan Earthquake,* USAID, Guatemala, December 1977, p. 132.

10. Toni Hagen, "Appraisal of the Situation in Guatemala", Caritas Internationalis, August 1976, p. 15.
See also Alan J. Taylor, *An Evaluation of the Problems Limiting the Promotion of Rural Development and the Effective Relief of Suffering by Catholic Relief Services – USCC in Mexico, Central America, Panama and the Caribbean with a Discussion of Policy Options,* CRS, New York, 24 September 1976, p. 252. Taylor reports that Caritas/Guatemala also tried

to limit the amount of food entering the country.

11. Froman et al., 1977 (a), op. cit., p. 24.
12. House of Representatives, 1976, op. cit., p. 34.
13. Decree 40-74; quoted in Froman et al., 1977 (a), op. cit., p. 25.
14. Sally Baker-Carr and Lyn Dobrin, "Double Disaster: Earthquake and Food Aid in Guatemala", *Food Monitor*, November/December 1978, p. 5.
15. "On the Receiving End", ibid., p. 6.
16. Roland Bunch, "Report on Aldeas with Recommendations for OXFAM-World Neighbors Kuchubal Project", Guatemala, (typescript) 21 March 1976, p. 3.
   In an interview with Bunch and William Ruddell, who also worked on earthquake related programmes in Guatemala, both men noted that the need for food aid ended after about two weeks. That, said Ruddell, "was when the farmers in the coop started telling us they didn't need any food. They said they had plenty of food in their houses". Bunch added, "Right. Most of the leaders I had been working with said, 'We don't need any food programs any more — you can cut the food aid'. But by this time, the PL480 food was pouring in from CARE and CRS . . . and was being handed out by their own staff and by the military, school teachers, Peace Corpsmen, and so on". ("The Relationship between PL480 Food Distribution and Agricultural Development in Guatemala," Antigua, Guatemala, (mimeo) 21 August 1977, p. 8.).
   Fred Cuny, another field worker, had a similar experience. He worked in most of the devastated area, and reported, "In talking with people throughout the country, food was always a major issue. When we went to talk to the people about housing, they would always ask, 'Are you going to bring in food?' And we'd say no. 'That's good,' they'd say, 'because we've got to try to sell what we have.' Everyplace, it always came up, though we were working in housing and didn't get into the details very much. But I know that the people, especially the farmers, didn't want the food coming in". (Jo Froman et al., "Edited Interview: Food Donations after Disasters and in relation to Agricultural Development, with Frederick C. Cuny, Executive Director, INTERTECT, Dallas", Antigua, Guatemala, (mimeo) 28 February 1977 (b), p. 12.)
   After the price of grain fell so drastically, one co-operative in the area decided to run a price-support scheme. With a grant from OXFAM of $100,000, it was able to buy grain at slightly above the current market value and within a short time, peasant farmers had sold 750 tons. Only when all the money had been spent did the project finish; the problem was not lack of local supply but lack of more cash with which to continue the purchasing. This is described more fully in Bunch and Ruddell, 1977, op. cit., pp. 14-16. Bunch concludes, "In other words, we were doing exactly the opposite of what PL480 was doing. We were creating demand, and they were reducing it". (p. 15) Further discussion is contained in Frederick L. Bates et al., "Emergency Food Programs Following the Guatemalan Earthquake of 1976", February 1979 (mimeo). Funded by the National Science Foundation.
17. Alan Riding, "U.S. Food Aid Seen Hurting Guatemala", *The New York Times*, 6 November 1977.
18. "On the Receiving End", 1978, op. cit.
19. Bunch and Ruddell, 1977, op. cit., pp. 11-12.

20. In interview with Tony Jackson, Port-au-Prince, Haiti, November 1978.

21. Stated by Mr John Shaw, WFP Senior Economist, on the BBC World Service programme "Talkabout". 4 June 1980.
The 1977 drought in Haiti provides an illustration of the difficulties posed by food aid even for emergencies. In addition to Title II aid, the US Government provided extra Title I (concessional sales) food to the Haitian Government. The agreement was signed on 13 April 1977 but, as an official telegram from the US Embassy in Haiti later explained:
"Corn did not arrive until September when worst of emergency was passing. Fortunately, the rains returned, better than normal, and this corn, which would have been treasure [sic] in a continued emergency, became a glut on the market and a burden to the GOH [Government of Haiti]."
Over 5,000 tons of corn were sold to a poultry dealer in Port-au-Prince, at two cents per pound (against its actual cost of over seven cents per pound). The telegram adds that the Haitian Government believed a market could be found for the estimated 4,250 tons remaining, as poultry feed in the Dominican Republic. (US Embassy, Port-au-Prince, Haiti, No. 2475, Sections 2(A) and 2(B), 22 June 1978.)

22. IPRA Food Group, *Circular Letter IV*, "Special Issue: Food Aid", (1/78), Zurich, 1978, p. 35.

23. Reported by OXFAM Field Director.

24. Catholic Relief Services/USCC, Zaire Program, "Situation Report on the Emergency Relief Program, Bas Zaire, October 18–December 3 1979", Boma, 7 December 1979. It begins:
"Since the emergency program became operational with the first arrival of Title II food commodities the latter part of July 1979, we are now able to report that considerable progress has been made in addressing the malnutrition problems in the project zone of Tshela and Lukule caused by the drought/famine of 1977–1978."
This report is an interesting example of how an optimistic tone tends to divert attention from the facts which are recorded. It was given to the author by a State Department official in Washington who said it illustrated a good food aid programme. In fact, of course, the food aid arrived much too late: it was delivered in July 1979 to relieve the drought/famine of 1977–78.

25. Personal communication from an EEC official, 18 Dec 1981. The author worked on the island from Nov 1979 to Feb 1980, by which month food aid was no longer necessary. For an interesting discussion about food aid in Dominica see J. M. Wit and P. Gooder, "Nutritional status of hospitalised preschool children in Dominica, before and after Hurricane David", *Disasters*, Vol. 5, No. 2, pp. 93–97, 1981.

26. Food was provided for 80% of the population for three months and for 60% over five months. The information for this section comes from Maria Colemont, a nutritionist and OXFAM project holder working in the Dominican Republic, who was interviewed by the author in November 1981.

27. Julius Holt, "The Helping Hand", *New Internationalist*, No. 53, July 1977, p. 14.

28. Ibid., p. 16.

29. European Communities, Court of Auditors, *Special Report on Com-*

munity Food Aid, 30 October 1980, p. 9, notes:
"Recently the Community authorised food aid operations of the so-called 'triangular' type. In these operations the goods are supposed to be bought in a developing country close to the one which is to receive the aid. Operations of this kind could play a part in encouraging the agricultural development of the country selling the goods. For its part the recipient country may receive aid better suited to the customary diet of its people. There are also savings in time and in transport costs."
The slowness of EEC emergency food aid operations has frequently been remarked upon and is the subject of concern to the Auditors and others. (See Andries Klasse Bos, "Food Aid by the European Communities: Policy and Practice", *Overseas Development Institute Review,* No. 1, 1978, and "Characteristics, Summary and Conclusion", in ISMOG, *Study of European Food Aid,* Vol. 1, ODI, London, 1976, pp. 18-19.)

30. Froman et al., op. cit., 1977 (b), p. 10.

31. One booklet does contain a useful set of guidelines for measuring tonnage needs. By using the method devised by the Center for Disease Control (CDC) of the US Public Health Department, it can be calculated that food aid requirements for a short period of time for 1,000 people "at risk" would be 1.05 tonnes of grain a week (the needs might change over a longer period of time). The booklet gives an example of how this method of calculating needs can lead to tonnages different from those requested.
"In 1975 the Government of Haiti requested food aid for a famine in the northern region. Very little information was given regarding the situation, except that over 22,000 tons of food-stuffs were required for a population of 300,000 people for a three month period. If the administrator is to assess the validity of such a request on the basis of such limited information, the CDC formula will prove practicable. Given that the weekly amount required for 1,000 persons 'at risk' would be 1.05 metric tons, the requirement for 300,000 people 'at risk' for a period of three months would therefore be:
$300 \times 1.05 \times 13 = 4,095$ metric tons of cereal.
The major discrepancy between the 'rule of thumb' assessment, and the actual requirement for food aid would suggest that the need for food aid may have been over emphasised. In such circumstances it would seem that there would be a good case for asking for additional information as to why the food aid requirement was so high."(" 'Rule of Thumb' Methods for Calculating Emergency Food Aid Requests", prepared by London Technical Group (Mark Bowden) for The Disaster Unit of the Ministry of Overseas Development, London, July 1976, p. 3.)

32. Cato Aall, "Disastrous International Relief Failure: A Report on Burmese Refugees in Bangladesh from May to December 1978", *Disasters,* Vol. 3, No. 4, 1979, pp. 429 and 434.

33. Ibid., p. 429.

34. Ibid., pp. 433 and 434.
Given the seriousness of the case described by Dr Aall, and that it happened recently in spite of so many years of disaster relief experience, it seems useful to quote here from the final section of his report.
"What can be done to prevent relief disasters like the one which happened to the Burmese refugees from May to December 1978? . . .

Whether it be from inside the UN family, or from one or more Governments, or from another third party, an initiative should be taken for an improvement in the handling of nutrition disasters and emergency relief operations (which so easily may develop into nutrition disasters). Below are mentioned some points for a possible programme.

(1) Establishment of an international advisory body with a pool of experts who could be drawn upon to assist in establishing and implementing some of the following points.

(2) Assistance to UN agencies, international and voluntary agencies or governments in drawing up actual relief plans; accompanying and assisting in initial assessment field visits, and later inspection visits . . .

(3) Assistance in running half-day or one-day orientation courses for heads of UN agencies and their top level officials to create insight and awareness on the major nutritional and logistic problems involved.

(4) Calling a conference (conferences) to discuss and establish certain disaster relief norms and recommendations regarding: dry rations (full rations, supporting supplementary rations); supplementary vulnerable-group feeding; treatment feeding for severely malnourished children.

(5) To establish or support one or more international school centres for research and training in nutrition disaster relief (operational integration of administration, logistics and nutrition) . . .

Such a programme or institution could become an independent third party for supporting and strengthening relief organisations, and also have a watch-dog function, mainly to help, but also to bark and bite if needed."
(p. 434)

Another important point is made in the "Afterword" by Stephen Green, UNICEF officer in Ethiopia, in Shepherd, op. cit. He notes that international disasters are like wars: international problems the resolution of which requires international involvement. Both points merit serious attention and should not be left lingering in afterwords or specialised journals.

35. Reports and memoranda on Karamoja relief operation, OXFAM, Oxford.

36. Quoted in Tony Swift, "The Curse of Amin Lives On", *Sunday Tribune*, South Africa, 28 December 1980.

37. Personal communication from Christopher Jackson, OXFAM Assistant Disasters Officer, 5 March 1981.

38. Trent O'Keefe, OXFAM/WFP Rehabilitation Officer in Karamoja, in interview with Tony Jackson, OXFAM, Oxford, 12 April 1981, (typescript), pp. 4–5.

39. Report by F. D. O'Hanlon, OXFAM/WFP Warehouse Manager, Uganda, OXFAM, Oxford, 1 May 1981, (typescript).

40. This is a well-documented risk associated with distribution of relief supplies. A useful set of articles on refugee settlements can be found in *Disasters*, Vol. 3, No. 4, 1979.

41. Amartya Sen, *Poverty and Famines*, Clarendon Press, Oxford, 1981, p. 137.

42. Keith Griffin, "The poverty trap", *The Guardian*, 7 October 1981, p. 10, in a review of Sen's book.

43. Joseph F. Stepanek, *Bangladesh – Equitable Growth?* Pergamon Press, Oxford, 1979, pp. 65–66.

44. Roland Bunch et al., "Problems with Food Distribution Programs: A case in Point", World Neighbors, Oklahoma City, 1978, (leaflet) p. 2.

45. Larry Simon, "Andhra Pradesh: Interview with Srikanth on the Aftermath of Cyclone", *The 7 Days Planner*, OXFAM-America, 1978, Issue 3, p. 1.

46. OXFAM Project UGA 54, OXFAM, Oxford.

47. The approach is fully discussed in Froman et al., 1977 (a) and 1977 (b), op. cit.

48. See, for example, Alan J. Taylor, *The USAID/Guatemala Lamina and Housing Materials Distribution Program: Ex-post Evaluation Report*, June 1977, a companion volume to Gersony et al., 1977, op. cit. AID also carried out a successful subsidised programme in Dominica after the 1979 hurricane.

49. Alex Rondos, "Problems that food aid creates", *West Africa*, 16 June 1980, p. 1055.

50. Maria Colemont, see ref. 26 above, 1981.

51. Caritas Diocesaine, Evêché de Port-de-Paix, Haiti, "Quarterly Report, July 1-September 30 1977," p. 1. (Translated by Tony Jackson).

52. "Quarterly Report, January 1-March 31 1978," p. 1. (Translated by by Tony Jackson).

53. "Quarterly Report, January 1-March 31 1978," p. 1. (Translated by Tony Jackson).

54. WFP/CFA: 11/4, "Annual Report of the Executive Director on the Development of the Programme: 1980," April 1981, p. 25.

55. Before 1976, the average PL 480 Title II tonnage to Guatemala was about 7,000 p.a. This went up to 11,600 tons in 1976–77 and increased to over 14,500 tons in 1978–79. Figures are obtained from Food for Peace Annual Reports on Public Law 480.

56. In interview with Tony Jackson, in Port-au-Prince, Haiti, 26 October 1978.

57. Personal letter from field worker, 11 April 1980.
    1979 figures drawn from Food for Peace, *1979 Annual Report on Public Law 480*, US Government Printing Office, Washington DC, 1981, Table 17.

58. IPRA Food Group, 1978, op. cit., p. 18.

59. Hjalmar Brundin, "Preliminary Report: FFW Secondary Effect Methodology Study", USAID/Dacca, (mimeo) 4 May 1979, p. 3.

60. Ibid.

61. David McDowall, "A case for reassessment", *Middle East International*, 19 June 1981, p. 11.

62. About 11% by weight of Title II (project) food aid goes directly to governments. Food for Peace, *1979 Annual Report on Public Law 480*, op. cit., Table 18.

63. European Communities, Court of Auditors, 1980, op. cit., p. 124.

64. Ibid.

65. Ibid.

66. See, for example, the "Statement by Mr Edouard Saouma, Director-General of the Food and Agriculture Organization of the United Nations, before the Committee on Development and Cooperation of the European Parliament," Brussels, 1 April 1980, as well as numerous publications by the FAO relating to food insecurity.

67. Figure derived from appeals reported in the British press, January–April 1981.
68. Statement by the Director-General of FAO, 1980, op. cit., p. 8.
69. WFP/CFA: 11/7, "Future of the International Emergency Food Reserve: Development of the Reserve into a Legally Binding Convention and Related Proposals", March 1981, pp. 6-7.
70. Ibid., p. 7.
71. Ibid.
72. Ibid., p. 6.
73. In 1980–81, OXFAM, for example, spent over £400,000 shipping rice to Vietnam, part of the funding coming from NOVIB of the Netherlands.
74. WFP/CFA: 11/7, 1981, op. cit., p. 6. The recommendation is proposed by the Director-General of FAO.
75. Otto Matzke, "Insufficient Control of Efficiency and Development Impact in the U.N. System: The Example of the Food and Agriculture Organization of the United Nations (F.A.O.)" (mimeo) p. 26. This is a translation of an article which appeared in *Das Parlament*, Bonn, 16 May 1981, (B 20/81). From 1962 to early 1974 Dr Matzke was Deputy Director, then Director, of WFP's Project Management Division.
76. The position of the US and EEC with regard to the IEFR is summarised in a WFP document (WFP/CFA: 11/SR.2, May 1981). The US "did not believe that it was necessarily desirable for IEFR pledges to be channelled exclusively through the WFP . . . since bilateral and multilateral food aid programmes both contributed to world food aid they should complement rather than compete with each other". (para 9) The EEC found the idea of a legally binding convention "at the present time, not so much wrong as irrelevant", adding that its regular contribution to the IEFR was being increased by 50% compared to 1980. (paras 23-24) The tonnage however only went up to 30,000 tons in 1981, a small amount indeed.
77. WFP/CFA: 11/4, 1981, op. cit., p. 23.

REFERENCES CHAPTER 3

1. Figures from Food for Peace, *1979 Annual Report on Public Law 480*, US Government Printing Office, Washington DC, 1981, Table 17 and *World Development Report 1981*, World Bank, Washington DC, 1981.
2. *World Food Programme in Egypt: Bread and Stones – The Salvage of the Philae Monuments*, FAO, Rome, 1979.
3. *World Food Programme: What it is, What is does, How it works*, FAO, Rome, 1981, p. 5.
4. *Employment Through Food Aid*, WFP, Rome, 1978, p. 12.
5. Ibid., p. 23.
6. *Overseas Development*, Overseas Development Ministry, London, September 1978, p. 4.
7. WFP, 1978, op. cit., p. 23.
8. Simon Maxwell, *Food Aid, Food for Work and Public Works*, Discussion Paper 127, Institute of Development Studies, University of Sussex, Brighton, March 1978, p. 33.
9. Ibid., p. 34.

10   FAO/AGS, "Les projets PAM-42 et TUN/71-525 et les perspectives de développement agricole du centre-sud tunisien", October 1971, quoted in a report of the Tunisian Ministry of Agriculture, Agricultural Planning and Development Office, 25 June 1973, p. 4. The translation is from Jacques Berthelot, "Food Aid through the World Food Programme in Tunisia: How to Carry out a Counter-Agrarian Reform," Rome Declaration Group, July 1979, p. 1.

11.   Berthelot, op. cit., p. 1.

12.   République Tunisienne, *Projet de développement rural intégré, Tunisie Centrale: rapport general*, Projet PNUD/FAO/TUN/72.004, Ministère de l'agriculture, Centre National des Etudes Agricoles, Ministère du Plan, Groupe huit, July 1974, p. 30. From Berthelot, op. cit., p. 2.

13.   Christopher Stevens, *Food Aid and the Developing World*, Croom Helm/ Overseas Development Institute, London 1979 (a), p. 129.

14.   Maxwell, 1978, op. cit., p. 40.

15.   Michael Scott, *Aid to Bangladesh: For Better or Worse?* Impact Series No. 1., OXFAM-America/Institute for Food and Development Policy, Boston, 1979, pp. 7-8.

16.   See, for example, Edward J. Clay, "Food Aid and Food Policy in Bangladesh", *Food Policy*, May 1979, pp. 132–133:
"A serious reservation about the overall impact of FFW concerns the longer term developmental benefits of rural works. A. H. Khan, architect of the Comilla rural development project, and many others, have questioned the productive impacts of rural works. There is also the problem of the acquisition by the rural elite of a disproportionate share of the benefits from infrastructural investment, particularly where earth works directly increase productive potential of the land."
Stefan de Vylder and Daniel Asplund, *Contradictions and Distortions in a Rural Economy: The Case of Bangladesh*, Swedish International Development Authority, 1979, pp. 198–199:
"The undoubtedly largest beneficiaries are the big landowners and associated interests among the rural elite. Among direct economic gains made by these groups we thus find land improvement and useful structures which more or less became the property of the landowners. . . . These direct improvements and increase in future productive capacity are also reflected in rapidly rising land values."
F. Tomasson Jannuzi and James T. Peach, *Report on the Hierarchy of Interests in Land in Bangladesh*, AID, Washington DC, Sept. 1977, p. 88, brings out this and other points:
"Such projects (e.g., the building of a farm to market road) provide income to rural workers for a specified period, but do nothing generally to change the fundamental economic conditions that produced unemployment in the first place. At the same time, such projects tend to provide long-term benefits to landholders who, in this example, use the road to gain access to local markets."

17.   Hjalmar Brundin, "Preliminary Report: FFW Secondary Effect Methodology Study", USAID/Dacca, (mimeo) 4 May 1979, p. 41.

18.   Ibid., p. 46.

19.   Ibid., p. 25.

20.   Ibid., p. 26.

21. Ibid.
22. Ibid., p. 28.
23. Ibid., p. 19. The project is described on pp. 10-19.
24. Ibid., pp. 37-38.
25. Jalaliddin Akbar, "Phulpur Thana, Rahimganj Union, Food for Work Project: A Case Study", USAID/Dacca, (mimeo) 1979, Appendix D, pp. 3-4.
26. Stevens, 1979 (a), op. cit., p. 116.
27. Ibid., p. 114.
28. Ibid., p. 116.
29. WFP/CFA: 9/10 Add. B1, Interim Evaluation Summary Report: Lesotho 352: "Soil and water conservation and road improvement", February 1980, p. 4.
30. Stanley J. Wolfe, M.D., "Evaluation of a Rural Tunisia Wells Project: Worthwhile Improvement or Edifice Complex?" M.Sc. dissertation, The Ross Institute, London School of Hygiene and Tropical Medicine, University of London, 1980, summary and p. 4.
31. Ibid., p. 16.
32. Ibid., p. 19.
33. Robert Maguire, *Bottom-up Development in Haiti*, IAF Paper No. 1, The Inter-American Foundation, Rosslyn, October 1979, p. 29.
    The problems posed by insecure land tenure and, therefore, the futility of trying to carry out land improvement programmes, have often been observed in Haiti. Adrian Moyes, *The Poor Man's Wisdom: Technology and the Very Poor*, Public Affairs Unit, OXFAM, Oxford, 1979, describes a contour-bunding idea that worked well in Guatemala but failed to make any impact in Haiti.
    "Too many people rented land in the programme area there, and they knew from first-hand experience that the landlords simply re-possessed any improved land — one of the programme workers has twice had land re-possessed because he improved it." (p. 22).
    Mats Lundahl, *Peasants and Poverty: a Study of Haiti*, Croom Helm, London, 1979, contains a valuable discussion of land tenure in Haiti. One section is of particular interest:
    "The absence of written deeds and of tenants' rights creates a potentially precarious situation for most peasants in the longer run, and this situation very often becomes acute when some innovation takes place that increases the value of the land. Alfred Metraux relates a case from the Marbial Valley:
    A peasant friend of ours had leased three-quarters of a 'carreau' from a townsman, at a rent of 40 gdes. Encouraged by the fact that for ten years he had been on excellent terms with the lessor, he started a small coffee plantation on the plot. The flourishing condition of this plot prompted a neighbour to ask the landlord to transfer the lease to him, in return for a rent of 60 gourdes. This suggestion was immediately accepted, and our friend was informed of the cancellation of his lease, in a note which offered no compensation whatever for the young coffee plantation he had started." (p. 603)
    The author adds that "anything that increases the value of peasant land is potentially threatening". (p. 604)
34. "Special Evaluation of the USAID/CARE Food for Relief Work Program",

USAID/Dacca, (mimeo) 8 April 1978, p. 22.

35. Hjalmar Brundin, "Food for Work in Bangladesh: Recommendations for Improved program Effectiveness". USAID/Dacca, (mimeo) 31 July 1979, p. 2.
    A comparable finding has been made for the massive FFW programme started in 1977 by the Government of India, using its own food stocks. See "Food for Work: Money Down the Grain", *India Today*, 16-31 May 1981, p. 122-123.

36. Ibid., pp. 5-6.
    Brundin adds that there is a possible variation of plus or minus 2.6 million in the 10.5 million figure, while for the 22.7 million figure, "according to CARE officials the measurements taken may be up to 20% off". (p. 6)

37. A fact noted, among others, by John R. Tarrant, *Food Policies*, John Wiley and Sons, Chichester, 1980, p. 265:
    "Finally, there are climatic limitations to the food for work programmes. The physical conditions mean that rural works can only be carried out successfully in the dry season. In Bangladesh and India, for example, this is the food 'fat' season following the main rice harvests. In the wet season the nutritional needs of the population will be higher, opportunities for alternative employment are lower, and the food for work programmes are not operating. The rural poor are picked up and dropped by such programmes at exactly the wrong times."

38. Christopher Stevens, "Food Aid and the Old: Doing Good by Accident", *New Internationalist*, April 1979 (b), pp. 21-23.

39. *World Food Programme News*, October–December 1979, p. 12.
    For further information on women's participation in FFW, see "Women in Food-for-Work: The Bangladesh Experience", an abridged version of a report by Marty Chen and Ruby Ghuznavi, WFP/CFA: 4/INF/5, September 1977.

40. *War on Hunger*, AID, Washington DC, December 1977, quoted in *Food Aid Watch*, Boston, (mimeo) October 1978, p. 4.

41. Glenn R. Smucker (ed.), "Food Aid and the Problem of Labor Intensive Rural Development", USAID/Port-au-Prince, (mimeo) 21 October 1979, p. 17.

42. Chavannes Jean-Baptiste, "Development or Dependency?" *Food Monitor*, May–June 1979, p. 11.

43. Calculated from the figures in CRS, Annual Summaries of Activities, Dominican Republic, from 1 July 1972 to 30 June 1978.

44. Tony Jackson, "Preliminary Report, PL480 Title II Food Aid to the Dominican Republic", OXFAM, (mimeo) April 1979, p. 5.

45. "On the Receiving End", *Food Monitor*, No. 7, November–December 1978, p. 7.

46. Eugene Linden, *The Alms Race: The Impact of American Voluntary Aid Abroad*, Random House, New York, 1976, p. 146.

47. Ibid., pp. 146-147.

48. Ibid.

49. David Cockley and Steve Mason, "Report of Agricultural Trip to the North West, 10-16 March 1978", (mimeo) pp. 2-3.

50. Ibid., p. 6.

51. Quoted in George Ann Potter, "PL-480 Foreign Assistance Food-Aid: Dependency or Development?" Testimony presented to the House of Representatives, Sub-committee on Foreign Operations, 4 April 1979, p. 7.

52. Claudette Antoine Werleigh, "L'aide alimentaire à Haiti", *Conjonction*, Port-au-Prince, Haiti, July 1978, p. 34, translated by Tony Jackson.

53. OXFAM Project VOL. 93, October 1980.

54. Ibid.

55. Smucker (ed.), 1979, op. cit., p. 14.

56. Werleigh, 1978, op. cit., p. 34.

57. Stevens, 1979 (a), op. cit., p. 117.

58. Smucker (ed.), 1979, op. cit., p. 56.

59. Ibid., p. 57.

60. Ibid., p. 55.

61. "Report on a Food-for-Work Project", *Food Monitor*, May–June 1979, p. 10. For a reply by CARE, see John McNamara, "CARE's Aid to Haiti: Food that Works", *Food Monitor*, January–February 1980, pp. 12-14.

62. Ibid.

63. Tony Jackson, 1979, op. cit., p. 5.

64. Community Systems Foundation, *An Evaluation of the PL 480 Title II Program in India*, Ann Arbor, Michigan, 4 June 1979, pp. 62-63.

65. John Osgood Field, "Development at the Grassroots: the Organizational Imperative", *The Fletcher Forum*, Summer 1980, p. 157.

66. Ibid., pp. 163–164.

67. Community Systems Foundation, 1979, op. cit., p. 62–63.

68. Food for Peace, *1978 Annual Report on Public Law 480*, 1979, p. 42.

69. *Employment Through Food Aid*, op. cit., pp. 35-37.

70. Ibid., p. 37.

71. WFP/CFA: 10/6 Add. C7, *Interim Evaluation Summary Report: Somalia 2294*, August 1980, p. 14.

72. Community Systems Foundation, 1979, op. cit., p. 55.

REFERENCES CHAPTER 4

1. Food for Peace, *1979 Annual Report on Public Law 480*, US Government Printing Office, Washington DC, 1981, Table 17.
The exact number of MCH recipients is given as 16,090,100 of which 66% are in Asia (10,779,800) and over half in India alone (8,156,000).

2. Ibid., drawn from Tables 16 and 17.

3. C. Capone, "A Review of an Experience with Food-Aided Nutrition Programs", *Nutrition Planning*, May 1980, p. xxii.

4. Mary Ann Anderson, *CARE Preschool Nutrition Project: Phase II Report*, CARE, New York, August 1977, p. 51.

5. D. W. MacCorquodale, AID memorandum, Dominican Republic, 2 March 1978, p. 2.

6. Clapp and Mayne, Inc., *Evaluation of PL 480 Title II Feeding Programs in Honduras*, Puerto Rico, 1977, p. 90.
The evaluators themselves did not see this as "reason to comment that

since it does not make a difference why not discontinue the program". However, since "the control group is no more under-nourished than those at the centers" and 43% of the children receiving the rations lost weight during the period, this would suggest that there is a need to consider alternative approaches and not simply to increase the supplements, as the report recommends.

7. "Encuesta Nutricional", Caritas de Guatemala, May 1977.

8. Denice Williams, Unpublished Master's Thesis, University of Ghana, Accra, 1977, p. 415.

9. Denice Williams, personal communication, 10 March 1978.

10. Food for Peace, 1981, op. cit., Table 17.
    Of the 8,156,000 recipients, 6,000,000 are enrolled on CARE programmes. The next largest distributor of US food aid is WFP, which has 1,585,000 recipients.

11. Community Systems Foundation, *An Evaluation Report of the PL 480 Title II Program in India*, Ann Arbor, Michigan, 4 June 1979, p. 12.

12. Ibid., p. 46.

13. Robert R. Nathan Associates, Inc., *An Evaluation Report of the PL 480 Title II Program in Morocco,* Washington DC, 29 January, 1979, p. xx.

14. Judith W. Gilmore et al., *Morrocco: Food Aid and Nutrition Education,* AID, Washington DC, August 1980, pp. 6-7.
    The ratios are said to provide "40 percent of the caloric, 70 percent of protein, and 73 percent to iron needs". (p. 4) The report also makes the following observation: "An interesting finding, contrary to what we would expect, was that CRS children who had been receiving only food for one or two years in 1975 appear to be slightly more malnourished (33 percent) than children just entering the program in 1978 (32 percent). . . . This minimal effect of food by itself on nutritional status supports the conclusions of other evaluators of feeding programs — that food supplements must be accompanied by education and other improvements in health and sanitation in order to maximize nutritional impact". (p. 6)

15. Personal communication of 12 December 1978, from Maria Colemont who organised the survey. For more details see the chapter on the Dominican Republic by Lindsey Hilsum in David Morley, Jon Rohde and Glen Williams (eds.), *Health With the People*, 1982, forthcoming.

16. Stewart Blumenfeld et al., "The Nutritional Impact of PL 480 Title II in the Philippines, 1970–1980", (draft) USAID/Manila, January 1981, Executive Summary, p. 3.
    In the summary, the evaluators note that "an analysis of 238 cases revealed that 53% showed improvement, 24% were unchanged and 23% regressed". (p. 2) In view of such findings, it is worth asking whether the improvement can be attributed to the supplementary feeding. As to what happens when children leave the feeding programme, the evaluators report that the data "cast doubt upon the long-term effectiveness of supplementary feeding. Again, the paucity of data preclude a firm conclusion in this regard but the fact that at Barangay Santa Cruz, of eight children who had 'graduated' from the program four months earlier, five had not gained any further [weight] and three had declined, and perhaps more significantly, of 14 'graduates' of the Santiago Nutri-Village, eight declined over the next few month and . . . with Aldana, two of 12 declined and none improved;

all these create a nagging suspicion that the activities that accompany feeding may not be very effective". (p. 33) They add that the "impermanence of the beneficial effect of supplementary feeding" has also been noted in *Alternative Nutrition/Health Intervention Effects and Cost-Effectiveness*, contract no. AID/ASIA C-1136, Virginia Polytechnic Institute, December 1980, p. 33.

17. Ibid., p. 43.

18. David McDowall, "A Case for Reassessment", *Middle East International*, 19 June 1981, p. 12.
The WHO document from which McDowall quotes is "Health Needs of Palestine Refugee Children", United Nations General Assembly, A/33/181, 17 October 1978, p. 4.

19. USAID Mission to the Dominican Republic, *Health Sector Assessment for the Dominican Republic*, 19 February 1975, p. 229.
The paragraph goes on to explain that the concept of food replacement "is supported by the very name of the program itself, 'breakfast program', which leads parents to believe food distribution is a meal in itself. In addition, meals are frequently served so late in the morning – around 10 or 11 a.m. – that parents may be actually reducing the amount of the family's food available to the child because they feel he or she has already been fed". The fact that such trivial factors as the name of the programme can affect its success serves to indicate the operational difficulties of food aid projects.
Anderson, 1977, op. cit., found the substitution rate in the Dominican Republic to be 69%. (p. 92, Table 37)

20. Anderson, 1977, op. cit., p. 37.

21. Capone, 1980, op. cit., p. xxiii.

22. Clapp and Mayne, Inc., 1978, op. cit., p. 41.

23. Anderson, 1977, op. cit., p. 26.

24. Robert Cassen, "Welfare and Population: Notes on Rural India since 1960", *Population and Development Review*, September 1975, p. 47, quoted in John G. Sommer, *Beyond Charity*, Overseas Development Council, Washington DC, 1977, p. 49.
It is now known that the post-war emphasis on protein requirements was exaggerated. "According to the 1948 figures, a child would need 15 per cent of his diet in the form of protein. According to the 1971 figures, 5 to 6.5 per cent energy/protein ration is adequate". (Colin Tudge, *The Famine Business*, Pelican, Penguin Books, London, 1979, p. 75.) About 60% of the food-stuffs released under Title II of PL 480 are blended and most of these are protein-fortified.

25. M. A. Moore, "PL-480 Title II Program – FY 1978" (draft), prepared for USAID, Dominican Republic, 21 November 1978, p. 13.

26. Comptroller General of the United States, *Changes Needed in the Administration of the Overseas Food Donation Program*, Report to the Congress, General Accounting Office, Washington DC, 15 October 1979, p. 58.
The full text reads, "Center administrators told us that the Title II food assistance was supplementing the diets of people who could not otherwise obtain the nutrition they needed. We noted, however, that Title II food was not distributed to MCH districts on the basis of the number of eligible

recipients. The MCH distribution official stated that the available quantity of food was simply divided equally among all districts. He said that until the Ministry completed its study of identifying the most needy areas, there was no other way to distribute the food". (p. 59)

27.   Anderson, 1977, op. cit., p. 63.

28.   Stevens, *Food Aid and the Developing World*, Croom Helm/Overseas Development Institute, London, 1979, p. 160.

29.   Ibid.

30.   Community Systems Foundation, 1979, op. cit., p. 40.

31.   Nathan Associates, Inc., 1979, op. cit., p. 101.

32.   Anderson, 1977, op. cit., p. 14.
Nathan Associates, Inc., 1979, op. cit., p. 77, also mentions that the MCH programme in Morocco focuses on 2–5 year old children instead of on the nutritionally vulnerable 1–3 group. This is policy decision taken to avoid 'competition' with a Ministry of Health programme aimed at the younger group.

33.   Checchi and Company, *Food for Peace, An Evaluation of PL 480 Title II, Volume One: A Global Assessment of the Program*, Washington DC, July 1972, p. 55.

34.   Ibid., p. 174.

35.   Community Systems Foundation, 1979, op. cit., p. 47.
The paragraph continues, "Either new delivery methods should be investigated, or the emphasis on the objectives of reaching this target group should be reduced". In other words, aims – and claims – should be brought into line.

36.   Figures taken from Food for Peace, 1981, op. cit., Table 17.

37.   Food for Peace, *1978 Annual Report on Public Law 480*, 1979, p. 41.

38.   Foreign Assistance and Related Programs: Appropriations for 1980, "Hearings Before a Subcommittee of the Committee on Appropriations", House of Representatives, Part 4, US Government Printing Office, Washington DC, 1979, p. 816.

39.   Linda N. Haverberg, "Some Observations of the Church World Service Nutrition Programs in Haiti and the Dominican Republic", *Case Studies of Development Programs*, CWS, New York, October 1976, p. 17.
The section is worth quoting more fully. "In general, the program lacks a clear direction and specific goals. It seems that operations have been established based almost exclusively on the availability of supplies (medical and food) and personnel . . . the majority of the 37 nutrition centers and all 3 of the raw food distribution centers . . . are at present merely *feeding centers*, and they constitute the major effort of the . . . Health and Nutrition Program. . . . Not only are there numerous problems in day-to-day operations, lack of adequate supervision, no formal educational programs within the centers, and no regular provision of medical services, but it seems that these centers are not even reaching the malnourished children in the communities. This conclusion is based on the finding that over 50% of the children currently enrolled in . . . nutrition centers are normal (as judged by weight for age)." (pp. 17–18.) The operational problems which are caused by the programmes being commodity-orientated and lacking clear objectives are reiterated in other US Government evaluations of PL 480 Title II.

40. Anderson, 1977, op. cit., p. 78.

41. Clapp and Mayne, Inc., 1978, op. cit., p. 24.

42. Food for Peace, *Fiscal Year 1975: Annual Report on Public Law 480*, 1977, p. 58.

43. Community Systems Foundation, 1979, op. cit., pp. 44–46.

44. Ibid., p. 45.

45. Ibid., p. 47.
    This is followed by the recommendation that "programs which do not do this should be actively discouraged".

46. Bantirgu Haile Mariam and Mario Maffi, "Evaluation of the Nutrition Field Workers Programme Supported by Save the Children Fund", Ethiopia Nutrition Institute, (mimeo) October 1979, p. 6.

47. USAID/Guatemala, "Survey of PL 480 Title II Food Distribution Centers and Storage Facilities", October 1977, p. 15.

48. Patrick Marnham, *Fantastic Invasion*, Jonathan Cape, London, 1980, p. 153.

49. WFP/CFA: 9/10 Add. 5, Interim Evaluation Summary Report 1, Pakistan 2237: "Supplementary feeding of infants, pre-school children, pregnant women and nursing mothers". February, 1980, p. 4.
    The following remarks on the educational performance of the project are also made: "Education of mothers in health and nutrition is part of the programme of the MCH centres. This is carried out mainly by talks, since no facilities are available for practical demonstrations. In some centres visual aids were available. No funds are available for purchasing local foods for demonstrations". (p. 4) Such observations do indicate that the educational component is not treated seriously, or even regarded as an integral part of the programme. It seems ironic that a programme in which WFP had already invested $17,489,600 worth of food (and a further $1,540,000 in additional expenses) could not find the funds to buy local foods for the purposes of demonstrating their correct use.

50. Merlyn Vemury, "Nutrition Education – An Important Aspect of CARE's Programming Efforts", in Kathryn Shack (ed.), *Teaching Nutrition in Developing Countries*, Meals for Millions Foundation, Santa Monica, 1977, pp. 146–147.

51. Anderson, 1977, op. cit., p. 78.

52. James Austin et al., *Nutrition Intervention Assessment and Guidelines*, Harvard Institute for International Development, Report Submitted to the United Natons ACC Sub-committee on Nutrition, June 1978, p. 9. One programme which does claim success with its education effort is described in Gilmore et al., 1980, op. cit.

53. G. H. Beaton and H. Ghassemi, "Supplementary Feeding Programmes for Young Children in Developing Countries, Report Prepared for UNICEF and the ACC Sub-committee on Nutrition of the UN", October 1979, p. iv.

54. "Conclusions and Recommendations of the Second Interagency Evaluation/Appraisal Mission for the WFP-supported Project Bangladesh 2226: Vulnerable Group Feeding in Distressed Areas", WFP, 13 February–4 March 1978, p. 25.
    A similar comment is made in the WFP/FAO audio-visual production

"Roadway to Development: WFP in Mexico". Item 47 reads, "since some of the foodstuffs are strange or virtually unknown to the village people, the government has sent a trained nutrition expert to explain methods of preparing food for the table". Item 52 shows the people how to use "... WFP rations with which they have now become familiar and have learned to appreciate". This kind of comment is not uncommon in WFP reports.

55. USAID Mission to the Dominican Republic, 1975, op. cit., p. 230.

56. Roland Bunch et al., "Problems With Food Distribution Programs: A Case in Point", World Neighbors, Oklahoma City, (leaflet) 1978, p. 2.

57. Much has been written about this subject. Among the documents are Mike Muller, *The Baby Killer* (3rd Edition), War on Want, London, 1977; Andy Chetley, *The Baby Killer Scandal*, War on Want, London, 1979; Dianna Melrose, *The Great Health Robbery: Baby Milk and Medicines in Yemen*, OXFAM, Oxford, 1981; James Firebrace, *Infant Feeding in the Yemen Arab Republic*, CIIR/War on Want, London, 1981.

58. OXFAM Project KEN 105A, Gill Tremlett, "Lake Kenyatta Settlement Scheme Report, July 1980".

59. Personal interview with Chris Dammers, OXFAM Field Director in Cairo, 8 June 1979.

60. Mariam and Maffi, 1979, op. cit., Summary, p. 1.

61. Ibid., p. 11.

62. Jon Rohde, personal communication, 27 May 1980.
For further comments by Dr Rohde, see Jon Eliot Rohde and Lukas Hendrata, "Development from Below: Transformation of Village-based Nutrition Projects to a National Family Nutrition Programme in Indonesia," in Nevin S. Scrimshaw and Mitchel B. Wallerstein (eds.), *Nutrition Policy Implementation: Issues and Experience*, Plenum Press, New York, 1982, and John Eliot Rohde, M.D., "Mother Milk and the Indonesian Economy: A Major National Resource", *Journal of Tropical Paediatrics*, Vol. 28, 1982, in press.

63. Roland Bunch, personal communication, 10 June 1980.

64. OXFAM, Annual Report: Zaire, 1979–1980.

65. OXFAM Field Report, 1 June 1979.

66. Caritas de Guatemala, "Segundo Informe y Evaluación del Programa Promoción y Nutrición, Julio 1978 a Enero 1979", (mimeo) p. 98. (Translated by Tony Jackson.)

67. Letter from a parish priest, Nueva Ecija, to CRS Head Office in the Philippines, 31 March 1979.

68. Tony Jackson, "Preliminary Report: PL 480 Title II Food Aid to the Dominican Republic", OXFAM, (mimeo) April 1979, pp. 8–9.

69. Miriam Krantz, "A Case History Replacing Imported Foods with Local Foods", League for International Food Education, *Newsletter*, Washington DC, March 1979, pp. 1–2.
The account of the project states: "The rehabilitation program has demonstrated to both mothers and other members of the family that milk powder and medicine are not necessary to treat children suffering from protein-calorie malnutrition. By feeding her child foods which she has selected and prepared herself, the mother can have the satisfaction of seeing her child restored to health in two or four weeks time." (p. 2)

70. World Neighbors, "Women Cut Malnutrition with Local Foods", *World Neighbors Newsletter,* Spring 1979. See also, "Topic: Food Self-sufficincy", World Neighbors, *In Action,* Vol. 12, No. 3E.

71. Thomas Marchione, "Food and Nutrition in Self-reliant National Development: The Impact on Child Nutrition of Jamaican Government Policy", *Medical Anthropology,* Winter 1977, pp. 66–67.

72. Beaton and Ghassemi, 1979, op. cit., p. 64.

73. Capone, 1980, op. cit., p. xxiii.

74. Ibid., p. xxiv.

75. Letter from a parish priest, Neuva Ecija, the Philippines, 1979, op. cit.

76. USAID Mission to the Dominican Republic, 1975, op. cit., p. 141.

77. Simon Maxwell, "Food aid for supplementary feeding programmes: An analysis", *Food Policy,* November 1978, p. 297.

78. Harvard Institute for International Development, 1978, op. cit., p. 8. For further discussion on *carefully controlled* health programmes, see Davidson R. Gwatkin et al., *Can health and nutrition interventions make a difference?* Overseas Development Council, Washington DC, February 1980.

79. Beaton and Ghassemi, 1979, op. cit., p. 44.

REFERENCES CHAPTER 5

1. Food for Peace, *1979 Annual Report on Public Law 480,* US Government Printing Office, Washington DC, 1981, Table 17.

2. Ibid.

3. Ibid.

4. *Food Aid to Education and Training,* WFP, Rome, 1970, p. 13.

5. John G. Sommer, *Beyond Charity,* Overseas Development Council, Washington DC, 1977, p. 49.

6. Food for Peace, 1981, op. cit. This figure is obtained by adding the 383,700 recipients in the "general relief" category to the 912,800 under "other child feeding" and "preschool feeding" and expressing the sum as a percentage of the total number of recipients – 66,360,889.

7. Christopher Stevens, *Food Aid and the Developing World,* Croom Helm/Overseas Development Institute, London, 1979, p. 138.

8. Ibid., pp. 138–139.

9. Food for Peace, 1981, op. cit., Table 17. Partly because it misses its main "target" group, school feeding in India was scheduled to be phased out by 1980, according to a US Government report written in 1976. However, the programme actually *grew* from the 1976 figure of 7,600,000 recipients to 9,400,000 in 1978–79. (See Comptroller General of the United States, *Impact of U.S. Development and Food Aid in Selected Developing Countries,* General Accounting Office, Washington DC, 22 April 1976, p. 14.) This is a good example of how food aid tends to become institutionalised, despite the evidence and even when governments plan to stop it.

10. Comptroller General of the United States, *Changes Needed in the Administration of the Overseas Food Donation Program,* Report to the Congress, General Accounting Office, Washington DC, 15 October 1979, p. 27.

11. Ibid., p. 26.

12. Stevens, 1979, op. cit., p. 139.
13. *UN Observer and International Report*, March 1980.
14. WFP/CFA: 11/10 Add. A2, Interim Evaluation Summary Report, Brazil 2325: "Nutrition Education and Supplementary Feeding in Primary Schools", 1981 (a), p. 7.
15. Ibid., p. 6.
16. Stewart Blumenfeld et al., "The Nutritional Impact of PL 480 Title II in the Philippines, 1970-1980," (draft) USAID/Manila, January 1981, pp. 110-112.
17. Ibid., p. 112.
18. Robert Cassen, "Welfare and Population: Notes on Rural India since 1960". *Population and Development Review*, September 1975, p. 47, quoted in Sommer, op. cit., 1977, p. 49.
19. Maria A. Tagle, "Operational Conflicts of Food Aid at the Recipient Level: Those Who Know Don't Plan and Those Who Plan Don't Know", *Food and Nutrition Bulletin,* United Nations University, July 1980, p. 12.
20. Simon Maxwell, "Food aid for supplementary feeding programmes: An analysis", *Food Policy,* November 1978, p. 294.
21. WFP/CFA: 9/10 Add. 1, Interim Evaluation Summary Report, Islamic Republic of Mauritania 055, "Institutional feeding", February 1980, p. 6.
22. Community Systems Foundation, *An Evaluation of the PL 480 Title II Program in India*, Ann Arbor, Michigan, 4 June 1979, p. 73.
23. Richard L. Shortlidge, Jr., "Assessment of the Educational and Health Impacts of the Mid Day Meal Program," USAID/New Delhi, 21 July 1980, p. 10
24. Ibid., p. 11.
25. WFP/CFA, 1981 (a), op. cit., p. 7.
26. Ibid.
27. Ibid.
28. Paul Harrison, *Inside the Third World*, Pelican, Penguin Books, London, 1979, pp. 318-319.
29. Checchi and Company, *Evaluation of the PL 480 Title II Program: Country Report: The Dominican Republic*, Washington DC, 11 May 1972, p. 28.
30. "CARE-Haiti, PL 480 Title II Feeding Program Plan for FY 1979," Port-au-Prince, 15 March 1978, p. 12. Since only about half the children of primary school age attend school in Haiti, this 4% figure represents only a tiny proportion of the child population.
31. Dr Guillermo Chihuahua, personal communication, 26 November 1976.
32. Paul Harrison, 1979, op. cit., p. 310. Chapter 17 of Harrison's book, "The Alienation Machine: the Uneducated and the Miseducated", gives a provocative analysis of the state of formal education in the developing world. On the general topic of education in developing countries, see the World Bank study edited by John Simmons, *The Education Dilemma*, Pergamon Press, Oxford, 1980.
33. Report on Interim Evaluation of WFP-assisted Project Arab Republic of Egypt 644: "School Feeding Programme", WFP, 1976, p. 5. 63% of

primary age children are enrolled and of these, 85% reach the final year of primary, i.e. 53% of all those of primary age.

34. Community Systems Foundation, 1979, op. cit., p. 74.

35. WFP/CFA, 1981 (a), op. cit., p. 6. Earlier, the report had stated that the number of school children benefiting from the WFP commodities "had exceeded the project targets, while the number of pre-school children is well below target. *However, each child is receiving much less food than was envisaged by WFP.* The reason for the low participation of pre-school children is to be found in the *lack of facilities and structure to distribute the food in some centres".* (p. 5 emphasis added) See chapter 7 for more discussion of the problems of administering project food aid.

36. WFP/CFA: 11/10 Add. A3. Interim Evaluation Summary Report: Central African Republic 478, "Pre-school feeding and community development", and 2006, "School feeding", 1981, p. 7.

37. Ibid.

38. Ibid. pp. 7–8.

39. WFP/CFA: 11/11 (WPME) Add. 1. Progress Report on Approved Project: Botswana 324: "Feeding of primary school children and vulnerable groups", March 1981, p. 4.

40. Tagle, 1980, op. cit., p. 10.

41. An interesting twist to the management problem comes from the Sudan where food aid for school feeding is sold at Port Sudan and the money used for local purchases of food. "In order to avoid the difficulties encountered in securing the transport of the commodities from Port Sudan to the provincial capital, WFP wheat flour is sold in Port Sudan at current local prices and the proceeds are turned over to the schools for the purchase of the required bread from the local bakeries." (WFP/CFA: 11/11 (WPMN) Add. 1. Progress Report on Approved Project: Sudan 531: "Assistance for School Feeding", March 1981, p. 3.) This circumvents the practical problems of transport and storage while keeping costs to a minimum. It also suggests that food is available in the country and that it is *money* that is required.

REFERENCES CHAPTER 6

1. Food for Peace, *1979 Annual Report on Public Law 480*, US Government Printing Office, Washington DC, 1981, p. 25.

2. Ibid.

3. Sumanta Banerjee, "Food Aid: Charity or Profitable Business?" *Economic and Political Weekly,* India, 7 February 1981, p. 176.

4. The publication *World Food Programme: What it is, What it does, How it works*, FAO, Rome 1981, states on p. 5 that, "The Programme's contribution is only a part of the total cost of a project, the remainder — often three or four times the value of the food input — being borne by the beneficiary country".

5. European Communities, Court of Auditors, *Special Report on Community Food Aid*, 30 October 1980, p. 34.

6. Food for Peace, *1978 Annual Report on Public Law 480*, p. 39, and Food for Peace, 1981, op. cit., p. 25. Although the comparison is not exact,

because the tonnages of the different food items changed from one year to the next, the trend here is clear.

7. Ibid.
8. WFP/CFA, 11/4 "Annual Report of the Executive Director on the Development of the Programme: 1980", April 1981, pp. 29-30.
9. Ibid., p. 30.
10. Food for Peace, 1979, op. cit., Table 2.
11. The figure is drawn from an AID draft memorandum of 8 March 1978 to the AID Program Officer in the Dominican Republic. The memorandum appears in the Appendix of Tony Jackson's "Preliminary Report: PL 480 Title II Food Aid to the Dominican Republic", OXFAM, (mimeo) April 1979.
    The $13,000,000 figure goes back only to 1968, whereas those from the Food for Peace document quoted above cover the period 1962-1978.
12. USAID Mission to the Dominican Republic, *Health Sector Assessment for the Dominican Republic*, 19 February 1975, p. 233.
13. From Jackson, 1979, op. cit., pp. 5–6.
14. Simon Maxwell, "Food aid for supplementary feeding programmes – An analysis", *Food Policy*, November 1978, p. 295, fn. 36.
15. Ibid., p. 297.
16. Ibid., p. 295, fn. 36.
17. Mary Ann Anderson, *CARE Preschool Nutrition Project: Phase II Report*, CARE, New York, 1977, p. 87.
18. Ibid., p. 91.
    Since the success in "reducing the rates of malnutrition amongst preschoolers" was shown in the same report to have been very slight, this remark is something of an understatement.
19. Ibid., p. 86.
20. See Chapter 4 and OXFAM Project DMR 13 for details.
21. Food for Peace, 1981, op. cit., Table 17.
22. Richard L. Shortlidge, Jr., "Assessment of the Educational and Health Impacts of the Mid Day Meal Program", USAID/New Delhi, 21 July 1980, p. 14.
23. Ibid., pp. 14-15.
24. Ibid.
25. Hjalmar Brundin, "Preliminary Report: FFW Secondary Effect Methodology Study", USAID/Dacca, Bangladesh, (mimeo) 4 May 1979, pp. 43-44.
26. Ibid., pp. 41-42.
27. Stevens, 1979, op. cit., p. 112, but see pp. 111-113 for the whole discussion, and p. 130 for the information about costs.
28. Ibid., p. 113.
29. Hans Singer, *Food Aid Policies and Programmes: A Survey of Studies of Food Aid*, submitted to WFP/CFA, March, 1978, p. 56, quoting Beaudry-Darisme and Latham.
30. WFP/CFA: 9/10 Add. 5, Interim Evaluation Summary Report: Pakistan 2237: "Supplementary feeding of infants, pre-school children, pregnant women and nursing mothers", February 1980, p. 4.

31. WFP/CFA: 10/6 Add. A1, Interim Evaluation Summary Report: Philippines 2318: "Assistance to elementary schools in Mindanao", August 1980, p. 3.

32. WFP/CFA: 9/11 (WPMF) Add. 1, Progress Report on Approved Project: Afghanistan 599: "Assistance to health centres, polyclinics and kindergartens", February 1980, p. 4.

33. Maxwell, 1980, op. cit., p. 296.

34. Ibid.

35. WFP/CFA: 9/10 Add. A1, Interim Evaluation Summary Report: Islamic Republic of Mauritania 55: "Institutional feeding", February 1980, pp. 1 and 5.

36. Ibid., p. 5.

37. Robert Cassen, "Welfare and Population: Notes on Rural India since 1960", *Population and Development Review*, September 1975, p. 47, quoted in John G. Sommer, *Beyond Charity*, Overseas Development Council, Washington DC, 1977, p. 49.

38. Shortlidge, 1980, op. cit., p. 15.

39. See David McDowall, "A case for reassessment", *Middle East International*, 19 June 1981, p. 12, for a strong argument along this line.

40. Stevens, 1979, op. cit., p. 60.

41. Gene Stoltzfus and Dorothy Friesen, "Voluntary Agencies in Calcutta", *Just World*, a report of an international assembly of development agencies, Calcutta, December 1979, p. 35.

42. Stevens, 1979, op. cit., p. 60.

REFERENCES CHAPTER 7

1. WFP/CFA: 9/10 Add. 5, Interim Evaluation Summary Report: Pakistan 2237: "Supplementary feeding of infants, pre-school children, pregnant women and nursing mothers", February 1980, p. 3.
Despite this, by July 1980, WFP was recommending that the project be continued for another two years and three months at a cost to it of over $29 million. (WFP/CFA: 10/8 (WPMP)) Add. 1., Project for CFA Approval: Pakistan 2237, July 1980, p. 1.) This second phase began in January 1982, with some of the managerial problems now reported to be largely overcome. (WFP/CFA: 12/12 (WPMP) Add. 5, February 1982.)

2. WFP/CFA:8/7 (WPMF) Add. 2, Progress Report on Approved Project: Nepal 2045: "Construction and improvement of mule trails and a jeep track in the hills", August 1979, p. 4.

3. Comptroller General of the United States, *Changes Needed in the Administration of the Overseas Food Donation Program*, Report to the Congress, General Accounting Office, Washington DC, 15 October 1979, pp. 55–56.

4. Ibid., p. 32.

5. European Communities, Court of Auditors, *Special Report on Community Food Aid*, 30 October 1980, p. 132.

6. Christopher Stevens, *Food Aid and the Developing World*, Croom Helm/ Overseas Development Institute, London, 1979, p. 88.

7. Ibid., pp. 88 & 104.

8. Ibid., p. 106.

9. Ibid., p. 142.

10. WFP/CFA: 11/10 Add. A2, Interim Evaluation Summary Report: Brazil 2325: "Nutrition education and supplementary feeding in primary schools", February 1981, p. 9.

11. WFP/CFA: 9/10 Add. C1, Interim Evaluation Summary Report: Sri Lanka 748: "Rehabilitation of village tanks", December 1979, p. 5.

12. WFP/CFA: 10/6 Add. C5, Interim Evaluation Summary Report: Senegal 2236: "Forestry works", August 1980, p. 5.

13. Clapp and Mayne, Inc., *Evaluation of PL 480 Title II Feeding Programs in Honduras*, Puerto Rico, 1977, p. 84.

14. Personal letter from field worker of 12 December 1978.

15. Marcon A. Moore, Administrative Specialist, AID, Memorandum to the file, Dominican Republic, 6 June 1978.

16. Hjalmar Brundin, "Preliminary Report – FFW Secondary Effect Methodology Study", USAID/Dacca, (mimeo) 4 May 1979 (a), p. 8.

17. Ibid., p. 23.

18. Robin J. Biellik and Peggy L. Henderson, "Mortality, Nutritional Status and Dietary Conditions in a Food Deficit Region: North Teso District, Uganda, December 1980", *Ecology of Food and Nutrition*, 1981, p. 169.

19. Hjalmar Brundin, "Food for Work in Bangladesh: Recommendations for Improved Program Effectiveness", USAID/Dacca, (mimeo) 31 July 1979, (b), p. 9.

20. David Henshaw, "The food aid fraud", *The Listener*, 21 August 1980, p. 228. This article followed the radio programme 'File on Four', broadcast on 20 August 1980, in which the effects of food aid in Bangladesh were examined. It included interviews with OXFAM field workers as well as other aid officials and recipients.

21. Brundin, 1979 (b), op. cit., p. 18.

22. Geoffrey Lean, "Scandal of UN's food aid in Africa", *The Observer*, 17 June 1979. (Quoting Dr Siegfried Bethke, formerly a senior executive in the WFP.)

23. Ibid.

24. Ibid.

25. In 1977, 10,000 tons of Title II grain were donated to the Government of Ghana. What happened to it is recorded in a report by AID's Area Auditor General – Africa, *Report on Examination of the PL 480 Title II Emergency Food Program in Ghana*, AID, Audit Report No. 3-641-78-1, 6 October 1977. One section reads, "We reviewed Government of Ghana records in Takoradi, Tamale, Bolgatanga, and four districts' offices and noted that the records maintained were incomplete and inaccurate. In Tamale, all original distribution records have been destroyed by Government of Ghana officials. Available reconstructed distribution records were of little value. In Bolgatanga, we noted that the source documents (waybills) did not agree with the distribution ledger and that neither the way-

bills nor the distribution ledger agreed with the distribution summary report. In the districts, we noted that the monthly receipt and distribution reports did not agree with the detail retained in the district". (p. 3) The audit concluded, "Undoubtedly much of the emergency food provided did not reach priority target groups of the affected population . . . we believe that a significant portion of this food was either diverted and sold or distributed in a way that was not condoned by the [AID] Mission". (p. 4) Tony Visocchi, "The follies of food aid", *The Tablet*, 7 June 1980, pp. 548–9, discusses the famine and EEC problems with its food aid.

26. Tony Swift, formerly Press Officer, OXFAM.

27. Reported by various agency officials to the author, Haiti, November 1978.

28. Personal communication from a German Government evaluator, 1981.

29. Stevens, 1979, op. cit., p. 142.

30. European Communities, Court of Auditors, 1980, op. cit., p. 124.

31. Richard L. Shortlidge, Jr., "Assessment of the Educational Health Impacts of the Mid Day Meal Program," USAID/ New Delhi, 21 July 1980. p. 4.

32. WFP/CFA: 9/6 "World Food Programme's Contribution to the United Nations Decade for Women: Priorities for 1980-1985", Report by the Executive Director, February 1980, p. 21. The extent of the commitment which WFP "does not have the capacity to monitor closely", is $2,086 million to 377 development projects during the five years from 1975 to 1979. (p. 2)

33. European Communities, Court of Auditors, 1980, op. cit., p. 107.

34. Ibid.

35. Shortlidge, 1980, op. cit., p. 15.

36. WFP/CFA, 9/6, 1980, op. cit., p. 21.

37. G. H. Beaton and H. Ghassemi, "Supplementary Feeding Programmes for Young Children in Developing Countries, Report Prepared for UNICEF and the ACC Sub-committee on Nutrition of the United Nations", October 1979, p. 58.

38. WFP/CFA, 9/6, 1980, op. cit., p. 28.

39. Community Systems Foundation, *An Evaluation Report of the PL 480 Title II Program in India*, Ann Arbor, Michigan, 4 June 1979, pp. 13-17.

40. Comptroller General of the United States, 1979, op. cit., p. 33.

41. European Communities, Court of Auditors, 1980, op. cit., p. 118.

42. Comptroller General of the United States, 1979, op. cit.

43. Alan J. Taylor, *An Evaluation of the Problems Limiting the Promotion of Rural Development and the Effective Relief of Suffering, by Catholic Relief Services – USCC in Mexico, Central America, Panama, and the Caribbean, with a Discussion of Policy Options*, CRS, New York, 24 September 1979, from when the programme began, in the 1950s.

44. Community Systems Foundation, 1979, op. cit., p. 1. According to the 1979 Food for Peace Annual Report (Table 2), over $1,006,000,000 of food aid had been distributed in India by voluntary agencies up to 30 September 1979, from when the programme began in the 1950s.

REFERENCES CHAPTER 8

1. See Bibliography for works on this subject.
2. Some examples, chosen at random from WFP project reports, will illustrate the way in which calculations are made.
    a) WFP/CFA: 10/8 (WPME) Add. 3. Project for CFA Approval: Comoro Islands 2545: "Multipurpose rural development", September 1980, pp. 15–16: "The quantities of cereals supplied by WFP will represent about 8.4 percent of average imports for 1978–79 and about 12 percent of local production. The amount of edible oil will represent about 2.3 percent of local production. Imports of oil have been very small and mostly related to food aid. . . [The Comoro Islands are] recognised as one of the food priority countries.
    Considering this and the small quantities involved, no adverse effect on commercial supplies or domestic production is anticipated."
    b) WFP/CFA: 10/8 (WPML) Add. 2. Project for CFA Approval: Brazil 2540: "Rural and community development in the Jequitinhonha Valley", August 1980, p. 17:
    "The WFP supply of cereals (2,880 tons a year) will be negligible both in relation to average annual imports as well as domestic production during 1976–78. . .These beneficiaries have very low income and their food intake is usually inadequate. The WFP supplies can, therefore, be expected to result mostly in additional consumption. Moreover, the quantities involved are relatively small; therefore, no adverse effect on commercial supplies or domestic production is anticipated."
    c) WFP/CFA: 11/14 (WPMA) Add. 1. Project Approved by the Executive Director, Angola 2480: "Assistance to kindergartens, orphanages and centres for physically handicapped", January 1981, p. 6:
    "The WFP supply of cereals will represent about 3.1 per cent of average annual imports during 1977–79, and about 1.1 per cent of local production. . . . The supply of pulses will amount to about 6.8 per cent of average imports during 1977–78 but will be negligible in relation to local production. . . . The WFP food supplies will be used to provide cooked meals and snacks, free, to beneficiaries under the project through kindergartens, orphanages, and work centres. These beneficiaries belong to very low income groups and their food intake is usually inadequate. The WFP supplies can therefore be expected to lead mostly to additional consumption. Considering this, and the relatively small quantities involved, no adverse effect on commercial supplies or local production is anticipated."
3. Siegfried Bethke, "Food Aid – A Negative Factor?" *Aussen Politik*, (German Foreign Affairs Review), No. 2, 1980, p. 192.
4. "Development assistance: is money more useful than food?" *World Food Programme News*, January–March 1981, p. 6.
5. Mary Ann Anderson, *CARE Preschool Nutrition Project: Phase II Report*, CARE, New York, August 1977, p. 40.
6. Ibid., p. 87.
7. Denice Williams, Unpublished Master's Thesis, University of Ghana, Accra, 1977, pp. 112–113.

8. "Evaluation of the USAID/Guatemala Supported Food/Cash Community Development Program", CRS Reference Project Number 76–44 (E) CRS, Guatemala, 15 April 1977, p. 8.
    Although people were able to lower their "market expenditures for traditional foods", they also had to buy sugar and cinnamon to add to the food aid: this effectively cancelled out part of their savings. (pp. 7–8)

9. Tony Jackson, "Food Aid Versus the Peasant Farmer", *Food Monitor*, May/June 1979, p. 8.

10. Ibid.

11. Ibid.

12. WFP/CFA: 8/6 Add. C.3. Interim Evaluation Summary Report: Bangladesh 2197: "Relief works programme for land and water development", August 1979, p. 6.

13. "Report on a Food-for-Work Project", *Food Monitor*, May/June 1979, p. 10.

14. Ibid.

15. "Interview in Guatemala with Francisco Batzibal and Benito Sicajan Sipac", *The 7 Days Planner*, Issue 3, OXFAM-America, 1978.

16. S. Bethke, "Notes on Future WFP Food Aid Policy in West Africa", WFP project review, 22 August 1977, p. 7.

17. Tony Visocchi, "The follies of food aid", *The Tablet*, London, 7 June 1980, p. 549.

18. Chiristopher Stevens, *Food Aid and the Developing World*, Croom Helm/Overseas Development Institute, London, 1979, p. 191. See pp. 188–195 for discussion on direct impact of project food aid on agricultural production.

19. Ibid.

20. Ibid.
    See also Food for Peace, *1979 Annual Report on Public Law 480*, US Government Printing Office, Washington DC, 1981, Table 17.

21. WFP/CFA: 9/10 Add. B1. *Interim Evaluation Summary Report: Lesotho 352: "Soil and water convervation and road improvement"*, February 1980, p. 5.

22. Figures drawn from Food for Peace Annual Reports between 1975 and 1979. Population figures for Lesotho taken from World Bank, *World Bank Atlas: Population, Per Capita Product and Growth Rates*, Washington DC, 1977.

23. Tony Jackson, 1979, op. cit. p. 8.

24. Service Chrétien d'Haiti, *Annual Report for 1978*, p. 8.

25. Tony Jackson, 1979, op. cit., p. 8.

26. *CARE Haiti Program Report 1978*, CARE, Port-au-Prince, p. 11. Three of WFP's warehouses were to be in the same towns as three of CARE's. One town, Gonaives, was to have *three* food aid warehouses, one belonging to WFP, one to CARE and one to the West German group, *Welthungerhilfe*. Sometimes the agencies compete not only with local farmers but also among themselves.

27. Ibid., appendix at end of Report.

28. Tony Jackson, 1979, op. cit., p. 9.
29. Ibid.

REFERENCES CHAPTER 9

1. Christopher Stevens, *Food Aid and the Developing World*, Croom Helm/
   Overseas Development Institute, London, 1979, pp. 198–199.
2. Community Systems Foundation, *An Evaluation Report of the PL 480
   Title II Program in India*, Ann Arbor, Michigan, 4 June 1979, p. 101.

APPENDIX

The following is a brief description of some of the countries and institutions that provide food aid. For much fuller accounts, see the books by Stevens and Wallerstein, listed in the bibliography. Individual agencies also provide annual reports etc.

UNITED STATES FOOD AID

The US is the biggest donor of food aid, accounting for about 50% of western donors' disbursements in cash terms in 1980. The US food aid programme comes under Public Law 480, the Agricultural Trade Development and Assistance Act, popularly known as "Food for Peace". The law was passed by Congress in 1954 and has since been amended on various occasions.

Broadly, the objectives of PL 480 are:

- to expand international trade;
- to develop and expand overseas markets for American farm products;
- to prevent or alleviate malnutrition and hunger throughout the world;
- to encourage economic development and improve food production in less developed countries, and
- to advance the objectives of US foreign policy.

In 1978-79 the total cost of the PL 480 programme to the US Government was $1,375,000,000. The food supplied accounted for 4% of US agricultural exports. There are three "Titles" or sections of the PL 480 Law which govern the distribution of food aid:

Title I

Title I of PL 480 provides for the concessional sales of agricultural commodities to "friendly countries". Agreements may be signed either for dollar credit with up to 20 years to repay, or for convertible local currency credit with up to 40 years to repay. There is a grace period of up to 2 years for dollar credit agreements and up to 10 years for local currency agreements. Down payments in dollars may be required. The interest rates are set by law at a minimum of 2% for the grace period and 3% thereafter. For the majority of Title I agreements the minimum rates have been used. Most of the foods provided are basic grains (wheat and rice). Edible oil, cotton and tobacco are also included.

In 1978-79 Egypt was the largest Title I recipient, accounting for almost 30% of the total in dollar terms, followed by Indonesia, Bangladesh, Korea, Pakistan and Portugal. Governments often sell Title I food through normal, commercial channels, gaining use of the cash resulting from the sales. However they are expected to undertake various self-help measures using these funds in order to qualify for participation in the programme.

Title II

This Title covers *donations* of food "to meet famine or other urgent relief requirements, to combat malnutrition (especially in children), and to promote economic and community development". In 1978-79 73% of Title II food in cash terms was distributed by US voluntary agencies, principally by CARE and CRS, 19% by WFP, and the remainder went to recipient governments under bilateral arrangements. 1,460,000 metric tons of food were provided for projects assisting 66,000,000 people in 80 countries. Wheat and wheat products were the major

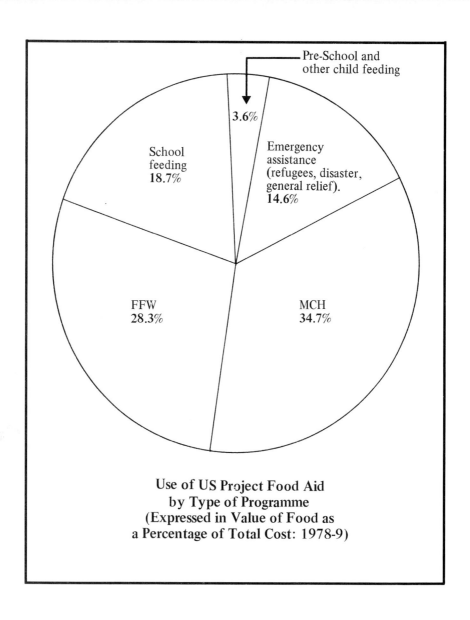

Pre-School and
other child feeding

3.6%

School
feeding
18.7%

Emergency
assistance
(refugees, disaster,
general relief).
14.6%

FFW
28.3%

MCH
34.7%

**Use of US Project Food Aid
by Type of Programme
(Expressed in Value of Food as
a Percentage of Total Cost: 1978-9)**

Food for Peace, *1979 Annual Report on Public Law 480,* US Government
Printing Office, Washington D.C., 1981, Table 16.

commodities donated, followed by corn-soya-milk and vegetable oil. Many of the food-stuffs provided under Title II are blended, usually soy-fortified, reflecting the emphasis on improving the nutritional status of the recipients.

India was the programme's biggest client in 1978-79, with over 29,000,000 recipients, of whom 9,400,000 were enrolled in school feeding and 8,156,000 in MCH. Bangladesh had the next largest number of recipients, almost 8,700,000, the great majority on FFW. The Philippines had almost 3,000,000 and Egypt over 2,000,000. Bolivia, Chile, Peru, Sri Lanka, Tunisia and Zambia all had over 1,000,000 recipients. CARE distributed food to over 30,000,000 people, WFP to almost 15,000,000 and CRS to 10,000,000.

In cash terms, Title II accounted for 40% of the PL 480 programme in 1978-79, including shipping costs.

A 1977 Congressional mandate established that a certain amount of food must be distributed each year under Title II. This is known as the *minimum mandated tonnage* and for 1981-82 stood at 1,700,000 tons.

Title III

In 1977 a new section, Title III, was written into the law. Under it, payments for Title I commodities may be waived if the money is used for development projects mutually agreed upon by the US and the recipient government. It is envisaged that this will become an increasingly favoured form of aid. It is known as the "Food for Development Program".

Cargo Preference Act

This Act requires that 50% of the PL 480 food should be carried by US vessels.

FOOD AID FROM THE EEC

The EEC as an entity is the second largest food aid donor after the US. In 1980 the value of its food aid amounted to $437,000,000, compared to the US total of $1,307,000,000. However, the EEC only gives grants and has no concessional sales programme. Its food consists mostly of cereals, skimmed milk powder and butteroil, and goes directly to governments or via international agencies, principally the WFP. UNRWA, UNICEF and non-governmental organizations also receive significant tonnages.

Food aid donated to governments is considered as a means of helping ease their balance of payments difficulties. Governments may sell the food and use the money from the sales as budgetary support. Among the major recipients of EEC food aid from 1977-79 were Bangladesh, Egypt, India and Vietnam. However, at the time of going to press it is EEC policy not to give aid to Vietnam. Operation Flood in India receives large quantities of milk powder and butteroil.

In addition to the above, some EEC member states donate food on an individual basis. In 1980 this came to about $280,000,000 in value and consisted mainly of cereals or of money to fund food aid programmes. All the aid is given as grants either directly to governments or via international agencies, particularly the WFP.

CANADA

In 1980 Canada provided $165,000,000 of food aid, both bilaterally and through international organizations, mainly the WFP. Almost all of it was on a grant basis.

JAPAN

In 1980 Japan provided $271,000,000 of food aid, of which $206,000,000 was

Food Aid from Western Donors, 1980, in Millions of Dollars

	Bilateral loans	Bilateral grants	Multilateral grants	Total
Australia	—	38.7	25.3	64.0
Austria	—	—	2.6	2.6
Belgium	—	5.2	34.1	39.3
Canada	2.5	76.0	86.3	164.8
Denmark	—	2.4	42.6	45.0
Finland	—	—	4.2	4.2
France	—	38.1	84.7	122.8
Germany	—	61.1	152.6	213.7
Italy	—	21.2	54.6	75.8
Japan	206.3	12.8	42.2	261.3
Netherlands	—	26.6	76.6	103.2
New Zealand	—	—	0.9	0.9
Norway	—	0.4	21.9	22.3
Sweden	—	7.7	39.5	47.2
Switzerland	—	15.8	12.1	27.9
United Kingdom	—	21.4	95.5	116.9
United States	687.0	471.0	149.0	1307.0
			TOTAL	2618.9

Of the food aid provided by EEC member states, the EEC as an entity disbursed $275,500,000 on a bilateral grant basis and $161,400,000 on a multilateral grant basis, for a total of $436,900,000.
Source: *1981 Review: Development Co-operation*, OECD, Paris, 1981, Table A.10.

on concessional terms similar to PL 480 Title I.

THE WORLD FOOD PROGRAMME

WFP was set up in 1962 by the UN and FAO. It is supervised by a 30-nation body, the Committee on Food Aid Policies and Programmes (CFA), which meets twice yearly in Rome to approve projects and to "evolve and coordinate short-term and longer-term food aid policies . . ." WFP's main aim is to stimulate economic and social progress by using food aid in development projects. Up to 1981, less than 20% of its resources had been distributed as relief.

WFP resources come from over 100 countries in the form of food, cash or services such as shipping. The US is the largest contributor of food, and the EEC and Canada are also important donors. Saudi Arabia is now a major cash donor. By October 1981, pledges to WFP of food etc. for the 1981-82 period totalled $759,000,000. For 1983-84 WFP hopes to raise $1,200,000,000 in food, cash and services.

WFP pays for the food to be transported to the borders of the recipient country (sometimes inland also). The local government is responsible for distributing the food and carrying out the projects. WFP has about 150 field officers living in the countries where it works.

CATHOLIC RELIEF SERVICES

CRS is the official overseas relief and development agency of the US Catholic community. Organized in 1943, it now works in about 80 countries in the developing world. CRS is supported by both government and private contributions. In 1979-80 $250,000,000 of its income came from the US Government and the EEC in the form of food and other commodities or to pay shipping costs.

CRS generally channels its assistance through local Catholic agencies such as local branches of Caritas.

CARE (Cooperative for American Relief Everywhere)

Founded in 1945 in the US, CARE is a private voluntary agency working in about 40 Third World countries. In 1980-81 it delivered PL 480 food to the value of $199,000,000, including shipping costs. 84% of its programme activities involved food distribution. CARE receives private as well as government donations and has information and fundraising offices not only in the US and Canada but also in some European countries.

CARE primarily disburses its food aid through local government institutions such as schools.

LIST OF THE MAJOR AGENCIES INVOLVED WITH PROJECT FOOD AID

Canadian International Development Agency
200 rue Principale
Hull, Quebec
Canada K1A 0G4

CARE
660 First Avenue
New York, New York 10016, USA

Catholic Relief Services (CRS)
1011 First Avenue
New York, New York 10022, USA

European Economic Community (EEC)
Food Aid Division
Commission of the European Communities
200 rue de la Loi
1049, Brussels, Belgium

US Government
Office of Food for Peace
Room 402 5A-8
Agency for International Development
Washington DC, 20523, USA

World Food Programme (WFP)
Via delle Terme di Caracalla
00100 Rome, Italy

Other UN agencies, particularly UNHCR (UN High Commissioner for Refugees), UNRWA and UNICEF also use food aid.

SELECTED BIBLIOGRAPHY

The present study involved the collection of hundreds of documents on all aspects of food aid. The following is a selected list of some of the most relevant writings on the subject. Further material is referenced in the footnotes.

1. **Bibliographies on Food Aid**

   Elizabeth Henderson, *Food Aid: A Selective Annotated Bibliography on Food Utilization for Economic Development*, UN/FAO, Rome, 1964, 203 pp.

   Hartmut Schneider, *The Effects of Food Aid on Agricultural Production in Recipient Countries: An annotated selective bibliography*, OECD, Paris, 1975, 41 pp.

2. **Food Aid in General**

   Sophie Bessis, "Le Sahel peut se passer de l'aide alimentaire", *Le Monde*, France, 9 November 1980.

   John Cathie, *The Political Economy of Food Aid*, Gower, Aldershot, 1982, 190 pp.

   Edward J. Clay, *Food Aid and the Economic Development of Bangladesh*, Discussion Paper 147, Institute of Development Studies, University of Sussex, Brighton, December 1979, 33 pp.

   Jonathan Fryer, *Food for Thought: The Use and Abuse of Food Aid in the Fight against World Hunger*, World Council of Churches, Geneva, 1981, 54 pp.

   "Food Aid", *The Economist*, 12 May 1979, pp. 100–101.

   Paul J. Isenman and H. W. Singer, *Food Aid: Disincentive Effects and Their Policy Implications*, IDS Communications 116, University of Sussex, Brighton, 1975, 19 pp.

   David B. Jones and Peter Tullock, "Is Food Aid Good Aid?" *ODI Review*, No. 2, 1974, pp. 1–6.

   S. J. Maxwell and H. W. Singer, "Food Aid to Developing Countries: A Survey", *World Development*, Vol. 7, pp. 225–247, 1979.

   Hal Mettrick, *Food Aid and Britain*, Overseas Development Institute, 1980, London, 1969, 124 pp.

   Alex Rondos, "Problems that food aid creates", *West Africa*, 16 June 1980, pp. 1053-1055.

   Hartmut Schneider, *Food Aid for Development*, OECD, Paris, 1978, 130 pp.

   Jack Shepherd, *The Politics of Starvation*, Carnegie Endowment for International Peace, Washington DC, 1975, 101 pp.

   Christopher Stevens, "Food Aid: More Sinned against than Sinning?" *ODI Review*, No. 2, 1977, pp. 71–85.

   Christopher Stevens, *Food Aid and the Developing World*, Croom Helm/ Overseas Development Institute, London 1979, 224 pp.

   J. R. Tarrant, "The Geography of Food Aid", *Transactions*, Institute of British Geographers, New Series, Vol. 5, No. 2, 1980, pp. 125–140.

Peter Taylor, "The Politics of Hunger: Cheap food is the major defence against political unrest", *The Listener*, London, 5 February 1981, p. 164.

Mitchel B. Wallerstein, *Food for War – Food for Peace, United States Food Aid in a Global Context*, MIT Press, Cambridge, Mass., 1980, 312 pp.

3. Project Food Aid

Cato Aall, "Disastrous International Relief Failure: A Report on Burmese Refugees in Bangladesh from May to December 1978", *Disasters*, Vol. 3, No. 4, 1979, pp. 429–434.

Mary Ann Anderson, *CARE Preschool Nutrition Project: Phase II Report*, CARE, New York, 1977, 169 pp.

Sally Baker-Carr & Lyn Dobrin, "Guatemala – Double Disaster: Earthquake and Food Aid", *Food Monitor*, November/December 1978, pp. 4–5. In the same issue, "On the Receiving End: An Interview" by Robert Gersony and Tony Jackson.

Sumanta Banerjee, "Food Aid: Charity or Profitable Business?" *Economic and Political Weekly*, India, 7 February 1981, pp. 176–178.

G. H. Beaton and H. Ghassemi, "Supplementary Feeding Programmes for Young Children in Developing Countries" Report prepared for UNICEF and the ACC Sub-committee on Nutrition of the United Nations, October 1979, 88 pp.

John Best, "Food Aid: For peace or patronage?" Reading Rural Development Communications *Bulletin 10*, University of Reading Agricultural Extension and Rural Development Centre, July 1980, pp. 6–12.

Siegfried Bethke, "Food Aid – A Negative Factor?" *Aussen Politik* (German Foreign Affairs Review), 2nd Quarter, 1980, pp. 180–195.

Siegfried Bethke, "Food Aid – A Negative Factor?" *Aussen Politik* (German Foreign Affairs Review), 2nd Quarter, 1980, pp. 180-195. No. 3, 1980, pp. 324–339.

Robin J. Biellik and Peggy L. Henderson, "Mortality, Nutritional Status and Dietary Conditions in a Food Deficit Region: North Teso District, Uganda, December 1980", *Ecology of Food and Nutrition*, Vol. II, No. 3, 1981, pp. 163–170.

Hjalmar Brundin, "Preliminary Report: FFW Secondary Effect Methodology Study", USAID/Dacca (mimeo), 4 May 1979, 52 pp.

Hjalmar Brundin, "Food for Work in Bangladesh – Recommendations for Improved Program Effectiveness," USAID/Dacca (mimeo), 31 July 1979, 27 pp. plus Appendix.

Roland Bunch, Mary McKay & Paul McKay, "Problems With Food Distribution Programs: A Case in Point", World Neighbors, Oklahoma, 1978, 2 pp.

C. Capone, "A Review of an Experience with Food-Aided Nutrition Programs", *Nutrition Planning*, May 1980, pp. xxi-xxv.

Prabhu Chawla, "Food for Work: Money Down the Grain", *India Today*, 16–31 May 1981, pp. 122-3.

Community Systems Foundation, *An Evaluation Report of the PL 480 Title II Program in India*, Ann Arbor, Michigan, 4 June 1979, 123 pp.

Comptroller General of the United States, *Changes Needed in the Administration of the Overseas Food Donation Program*, Report to the Congress, General Accounting Office, Washington DC, 15 October 1979, 91 pp.

John Osgood Field, "Development at the Grassroots: The Organizational Imperative", *The Fletcher Forum*, Summer 1980, pp. 145-164.

"Food Aid: The Case of Haiti", three articles in *Food Monitor*, May/June 1979, pp. 8-11: Tony Jackson, "Food Aid Versus the Peasant Farmer", "Report on a Food-for-Work Project" by a development worker, and "Development or Dependency?" by Chavannes Jean-Baptiste, Director of Caritas, Diocese of Hinche.

Food for Peace: An Evaluation of PL 480 Title II, Vol. 1, "A Global Assessment of the Programme", Checchi & Company, Washington DC, July 1972, pp. 201, plus Appendices.

Davidson R. Gwatkin et al., *Can Health and Nutrition Interventions Make a Difference?* Monograph No. 13, Overseas Development Council, Washington DC, 1980, 76 pp.

Geoffrey Lean, "Scandal of UN's food aid in Africa", *The Observer*, 17 June 1979.

John Madeley, "Tunisian olives: development or dependence?", *Earthscan*, London, 5 August 1980.

Otto Matzke, "Shortcomings of Food Aid: practical experience of the World Food Programme", a translation of "Schwachstellen der Nahrungsmittelhilfe", *Neue Zurcher Zeitung*, 28 December 1978.

Simon Maxwell, *Food Aid, Food for Work and Public Works*, Discussion Paper 127, Institute of Development Studies, University of Sussex, Brighton, March 1978, 47 pp.

Simon Maxwell, "Food aid for supplementary feeding programmes: An analysis", *Food Policy*, November 1978, pp. 289-298.

Caroline Moorehead, "Experts question benefits of food aid"; "Disaster relief often inappropriate and ineffective"; "Subsidised food can be best way to combat famine", *The Times*, 28, 29 & 30 April 1981.

Barry Newman, "World Hunger — Graft and Inefficiency in Bangladesh Subvert Food-for-Work Plans", *The Wall Street Journal*, 20 April 1981.

Peasant Perceptions: Famine, Bangladesh Rural Advancement Committee (BRAC), Dacca, Bangladesh, July 1979, 28 pp.

Alan Riding, "U.S. Food Aid Seen Hurting Guatemala", *The New York Times*, 6 November 1977.

Peter Stalker, "Food Confusion", *New Internationalist*, December 1979, pp. 22-24.

Richard L. Shortlidge, Jr., "Assessment of the Educational and Health Impacts of the Mid Day Meal Program", USAID, New Delhi, 21 July 1980, 33 pp.

Maria A. Tagle, "Operational Conflicts of Food Aid at the Recipient Level: Those Who Know Don't Plan and Those Who Plan Don't Know", *Food and Nutrition Bulletin*, the United Nations University, Tokyo, July 1980, pp. 5-15.

John Taylor et al., "The Fight Over Food Aid", Newsweek, 27 April 1981, pp. 38-39.

Tony Visocchi, "The follies of food aid", *The Tablet*, London, 7 June 1980, pp. 548–9.

Mark Winiarski, three articles under the general title "CRS: Image vs Reality"; "Morale, funding woes hit Catholic Relief"; "Staff lament bosses' 'errors in judgment' "; "Government pays CRS overhead", *National Catholic Reporter*, Kansas City, 28 September, 5 and 12 October 1979. *The National Catholic Reporter* of 5 October also carries an editorial entitled "The $300 million dump truck".

4. **Food Aid from the EEC**

Communication from the Commission to the Council concerning Food Aid Programmes for 1981, Commission of the European Communities, COM (81) 41 Final, Brussels, 11 February 1981, 78 pp. (A document produced yearly with details of the proposed EEC food aid programme).

European Communities, Court of Auditors, *Special Report on Community Food Aid*, 30 October 1980, 148 pp.

Annex to the report of Mr Ferrero on the European Community's contribution to the campaign against hunger in the world, European Parliament Working Documents 1980–1981, 5 September 1980, Document 1–341/80/ Annex 1, 209 pp. The working document, "An effective food aid policy that takes into account the needs of hunger-striken countries and peoples – emergency aid", drawn up by Mrs K. Focke (pp. 55–90) is of special interest.

ISMOG, University of Amsterdam, *Etude de l'Aide Alimentaire des Communautés Européenes*, Amsterdam, 1977.

Andries Klaasse Bos, "Food aid by the European Communities: Policy and Practice", *ODI Review*, No. 1, 1978, pp. 38–52.

5. **US Food Aid, with Particular Reference to Titles I and III**

Official Documents

Facts and figures on US food aid are to be found in the annual Food for Peace reports on Public Law 480, published by the U.S. Government Printing Office. Information on the legislation of US food aid may be found in:

Agricultural Trade Development and Assistance Act of 1964 and Amendments, Gilman G. Udell, Superintendent, Document Room, House of Representatives, 1976, 66 pp.

American Foreign Food Assistance – Public Law 480 and Related Materials, Committee on Agriculture and Forestry, United States Senate, 13 August 1976, 43 pp.

Food for Peace, 1954–1978 – Major Changes in Legislation, Congressional Research Service, the Library of Congress, 26 April 1979, 59 pp.

Official analyses on US food aid are produced periodically by the General Accounting Office (GAO), Washington DC. Among them are:

Comptroller General of the United States, *Disincentives to Agricultural Production in Developing Countries*, Report to the Congress, GAO, 26 November 1975, 117 pp.

Comptroller General of the United States, *Impact of U.S. Development and Food Aid in Selected Developing Countries*, GAO, 22 April 1976, 42 pp.

Comptroller General of the United States, *Search for Options in the Troubled Food-for-Peace Program in Zaire*, Report to the Subcommittee on Africa, House Committee on Foreign Affairs, GAO, 22 February 1980, 35 pp.

Comptroller General of the United States, *Food for Development Program: Constrained by Unresolved Management and Policy Questions*, Report to the Congress, GAO, 23 June 1981, 55 pp.

Other Material

James E. Austin and Mitchel B. Wallerstein, "Reformulating US Food Aid Policy for Development", *World Development*, Vol. 7, 1979, pp. 635–646.

Leonard Dudley and Roger J. Sandilands, "The Side Effects of Foreign Aid: The Case of Public Law 480 Wheat in Colombia", *Economic Development and Cultural Change*, Jan 1975, pp. 325–336.

Betsy Hartmann and James Boyce, *Needless Hunger: Voices from a Bangladesh Village*, Institute for Food and Development Policy, San Francisco, 1979, 72 pp.

Donald F. McHenry and Kai Bird, "Food Bungle in Bangladesh", *Foreign Policy*, Summer 1977, pp. 72–88.

James Morrell, "The Big Stick: The Use and Abuse of Food Aid", *Food Monitor*, December 1977.

Emma Rothschild, "Is it time to end Food for Peace?" *The New York Times Magazine*, 13 March 1977, pp. 43–48.

Theodore W. Schultz, "Value of U.S. Farm Surpluses to Underdeveloped Countries", *Journal of Farm Economics*, Dec 1960, pp. 1019–1030.

6. **Dairy Aid**

The EEC is by far the largest donor of dairy aid, both as skimmed milk powder and butteroil, much of it distributed through the WFP. "Operation Flood" in India is often quoted as a model for the use of milk powder but is not dealt with in this report as the milk powder is not used as *project* food aid. The following documents look at dairy aid, some at "Operation Flood" in particular. For reference to books discussing the use of milk powder in general in the Third World, see footnote 58 to Chapter 4.

John Clark, "Dairy aid: from Europe with love?", Earthscan, London, 29 August 1980, 6 pp.

John Clark, *Milking Whom? A Study of Europe's Leading Agricultural Sector, and Its Effects on European and Third World Food Systems*, International Coalition for Development Action, London 1979, 71 pp.

John Clark, "Concern About EEC Dairy Aid", OXFAM, Oxford, 1980, 7 pp. plus Appendices (mimeo).

Raymond Crotty, "How Europe's milk is becoming India's poison", *The Times*, 6 May 1977.

Raymond Crotty, *Cattle, Economics and Development*, Commonwealth Agricultural Bureaux, Slough, England, 1980, 253 pp.

Bharat Dogra, *The Milk Muddle: Are national interests in dairying being sabotaged?* C–1/51 Janakpuri, New Delhi, 110058, April 1980, 48 pp.

Bernard Kervyn, *From Dairy Aid to Milk Powder Business: The Dairy Sector in Bangladesh*, Community Development Library, GPO Box 235, Dacca 2, 1981, 50 pp.

Handle with Care: Skim Milk Aid to Developing Countries, The North-South Institute, Ottawa, 1979, 80 pp.

John Torode, "Operation Flood", *WFP News*, Oct-Dec 81, pp. 2-4, (first of a series).

WFP/CFA: 12/7 Add. C6, Summary Terminal Evaluation Report, India 618: "Milk marketing and dairy development, Operation Flood 1", September 1981, 30 pp.

The National Dairy Development Board ("Operation Flood") publishes an Annual Report, available from P.O. Box 40, Anand 388011, India.

7. **Radio and Television Coverage of Food Aid**

"The Politics of Hunger", BBC TV, *Panorama*, 2 February 1981, produced by Jonathan Holmes, looks at food aid in Mali.

"Food Aid: What's in it for U.S.?" PBS TV, 21 October 1981, produced by William Cran and Stephanie Tepper, (WORLD/WGBH TV, Boston).

"The Food Aid Fraud", BBC radio *File on 4*, 20 August 1980, produced by Gerry Northam, reports on food aid to Bangladesh.

(Films, tape and transcripts available from relevant office).